STAR WARS

THE LAST JEDI

INCREDIBLE CROSS-SECTIONS

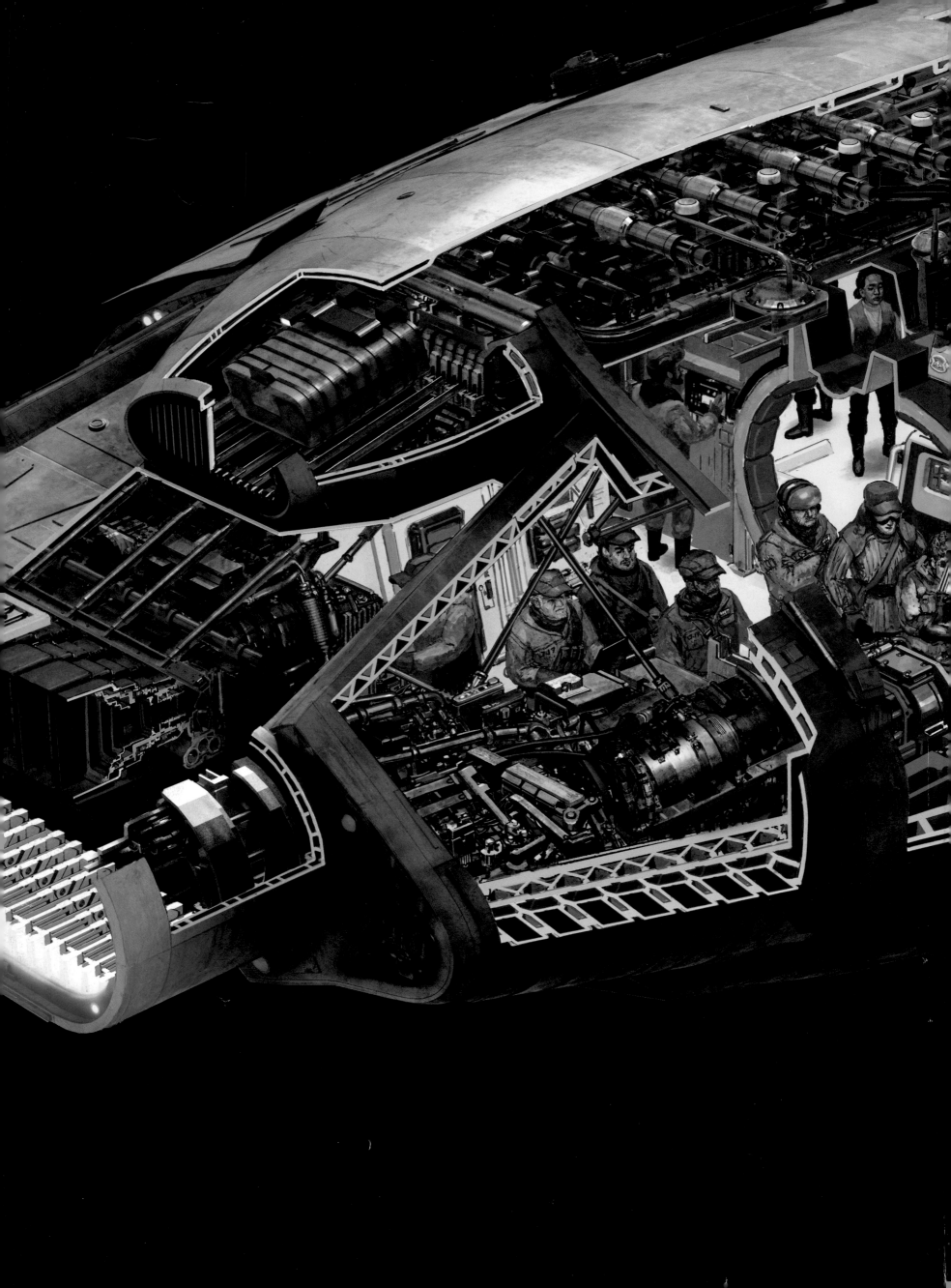

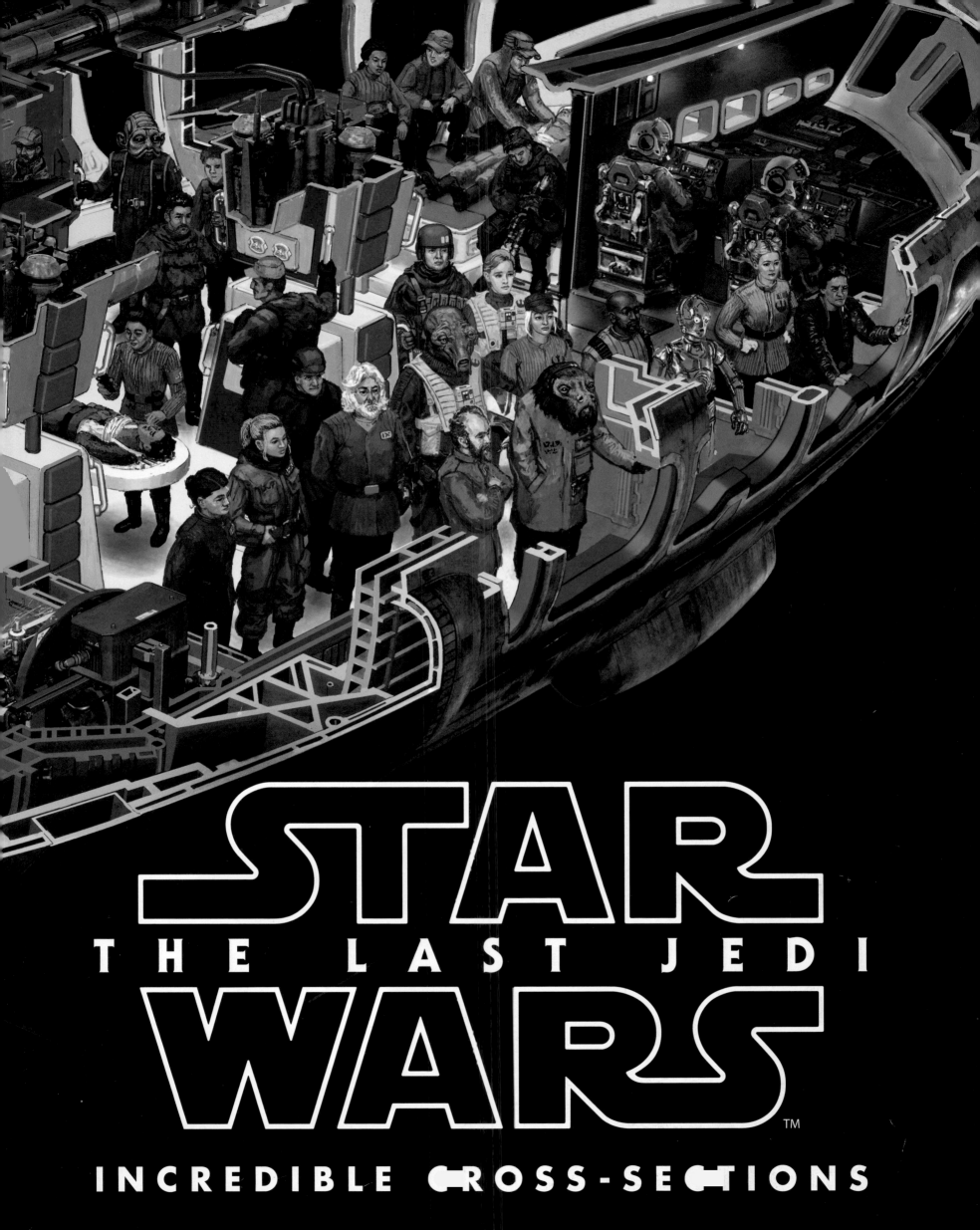

STAR WARS
THE LAST JEDI
WARS

INCREDIBLE CROSS-SECTIONS

ILLUSTRATED BY KEMP REMILLARD • WRITTEN BY JASON FRY

CONTENTS

INTRODUCTION

STARKILLER BASE IS NO MORE, but the galaxy still faces grave peril after the First Order's deadly assault on Hosnian Prime. This sneak attack incinerated the New Republic capital, its leadership and key elements of its fleet. With the galaxy's far-flung worlds still reeling and off balance, a war fleet commanded by General Hux follows the Resistance's starfighters back to their base on D'Qar, hoping to avenge the defeat at Starkiller Base. Hux knows it is vital that they put an end to the Resistance quickly, before opposition to the First Order can be organised. Although General Leia Organa and her allies escape from Hux's assault, Supreme Leader Snoke soon joins the pursuit of the fleeing Resistance, revealing his mighty flagship, and a fleet of secretly built Star Destroyers. Snoke hopes to witness Organa's demise, but is also mindful of reverberations in the Force – ripples caused by events on a lost world, where a desperate seeker has discovered the refuge of the last Jedi.

GALACTIC FACTIONS

THE RESISTANCE

The Resistance's predicament is dire. The New Republic is all but destroyed, and the First Order has unleashed its war machine to seek revenge for the raid on Starkiller Base. Leia Organa and fellow Resistance leaders fight back with a ragtag assembly of ships salvaged from New Republic scrapyards, lent by sympathetic allies, converted from civilian models or left over from the days of the Rebel Alliance. With the galaxy's independent systems fearful of being drawn into renewed conflict, the Resistance stands alone against the First Order – making its brave pilots the last defence against a new era of tyranny.

THE FIRST ORDER

Even as he fought to destroy the Alliance, Emperor Palpatine was seeking answers to the oldest riddles of the Force among the mysterious star systems of the galaxy's Unknown Regions. Palpatine ordered Imperial scouts to blaze hyperspace trails beyond the frontier and constructed a vast network of labs, shipyards and bases as part of his plan to expand the Empire once the rebel threat had been quelled. The First Order inherited these facilities, using them to make advances in military technology and create huge fleets and armies. It then awaited the right moment to unleash its fury on the New Republic and reclaim dominion over the galaxy.

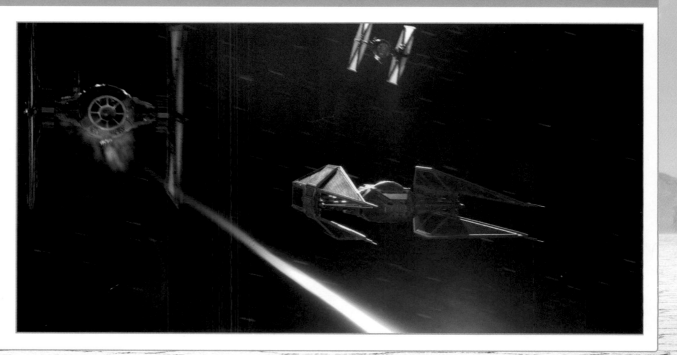

ATTACK RUN

On board the Resistance bomber *Crimson Hailstorm* bombardier Edon Kappehl prepares to target the First Order fleet. Edon is aware that even a single hit on its bomb bay could instantly vaporise his ship and its crew.

THE *RADDUS*

THE PRIDE OF the Resistance, the *Raddus* is a mobile command centre for General Leia Organa and a symbol of the struggle for galactic freedom. Its name celebrates one of the Rebellion's earliest heroes, while its construction incorporates contributions from different shipyards and species. The *Raddus* serves as a carrier for the Resistance's hastily reconstituted starfighter corps. It is also the flagship of the ragged task force that flees D'Qar, just ahead of the First Order fleet bent on avenging the destruction of Starkiller Base. The fate of the Resistance and the dream of a free and peaceful galaxy both rest with this wounded warship. It races through space with an enigmatic commander at its helm and a restive crew desperately hoping that a safe haven can be found.

RAISED SHIELDS

The advanced deflector shields that cocoon the *Raddus* are an experimental design, capable of sustaining huge amounts of damage before failing. Though their heavy pummelling by the First Order makes structural damage inevitable, most other ships would have been destroyed long before this point.

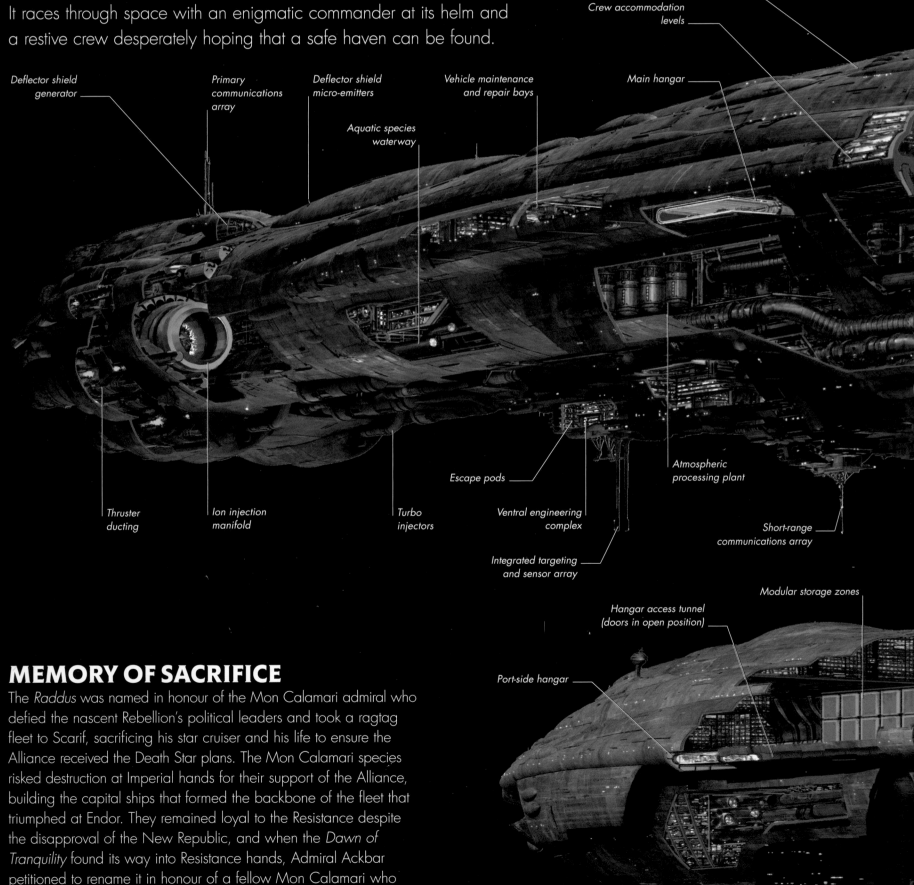

Deflector shield generator

Primary communications array

Deflector shield micro-emitters

Aquatic species waterway

Vehicle maintenance and repair bays

Durasteel hull plating

Crew accommodation levels

Main hangar

Thruster ducting

Ion injection manifold

Turbo injectors

Escape pods

Ventral engineering complex

Integrated targeting and sensor array

Atmospheric processing plant

Short-range communications array

Port-side hangar

Hangar access tunnel (doors in open position)

Modular storage zones

Ventral crew decks

MEMORY OF SACRIFICE

The *Raddus* was named in honour of the Mon Calamari admiral who defied the nascent Rebellion's political leaders and took a ragtag fleet to Scarif, sacrificing his star cruiser and his life to ensure the Alliance received the Death Star plans. The Mon Calamari species risked destruction at Imperial hands for their support of the Alliance, building the capital ships that formed the backbone of the fleet that triumphed at Endor. They remained loyal to the Resistance despite the disapproval of the New Republic, and when the *Dawn of Tranquility* found its way into Resistance hands, Admiral Ackbar petitioned to rename it in honour of a fellow Mon Calamari who had chosen to fight against seemingly insurmountable odds.

NEW OWNERSHIP

Originally named the *Dawn of Tranquility*, the *Raddus* once formed part of the New Republic's home fleet, but was decommissioned early – a move made with one eye on treaties limiting heavy warships and another on being able to reduce navy personnel. For the MC85 line, the Mon Calamari worked with the venerable Corellian Engineering Corporation to create interiors more amenable to non-amphibious crews. This has allowed the Resistance to avoid costly retrofits.

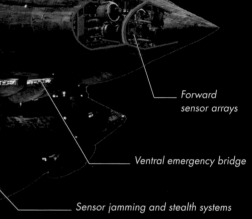

Concealed turbolaser battery

Turbolaser targeting array

Leia Organa's quarters

Tractor beam emitter

Primary command bridge

Starboard main turbolift shaft

Turbolaser cannon blister

Forward sensor arrays

Ventral emergency bridge

Sensor jamming and stealth systems

Ion scoop particle collector

Atmosphere ducts

Auxiliary decks are currently abandoned

Fuel storage

CHANGE OF COMMAND

After a First Order attack kills much of the *Raddus'* command crew and leaves General Organa badly injured, Vice Admiral Amilyn Holdo transfers her flag from the *Ninka* and assumes command of the Resistance fleet. With the *Raddus'* primary bridge in ruins, Holdo directs operations from the cruiser's ventral emergency bridge.

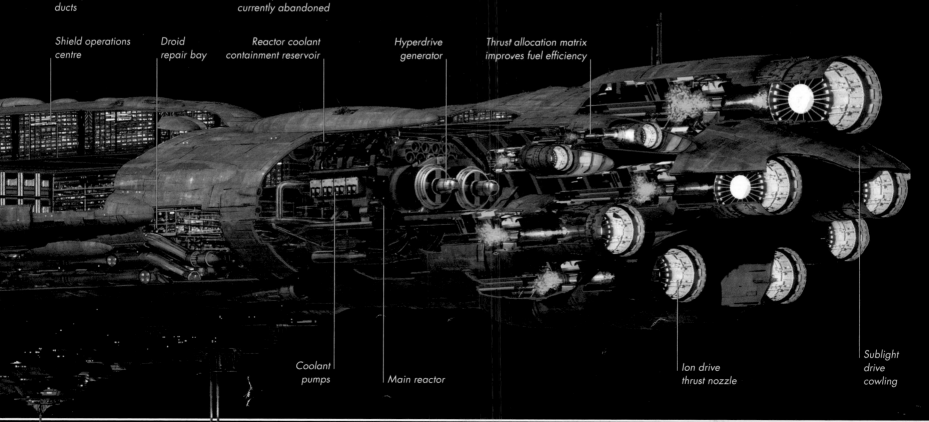

Shield operations centre

Droid repair bay

Reactor coolant containment reservoir

Hyperdrive generator

Thrust allocation matrix improves fuel efficiency

Coolant pumps

Main reactor

Ion drive thrust nozzle

Sublight drive cowling

RESISTANCE CAPITAL SHIPS

THE RESISTANCE FLEET is barely worthy of the name: four capital ships, a handful of support craft and a few squadrons of bombers and starfighters. But Leia Organa's movement has always relied on assets not recorded in an order of battle – local allies, a capable spy network and clandestine support from the New Republic allowed it to keep tabs on the First Order. As Organa and her old friend Admiral Holdo remind impatient Resistance commanders, the Rebel Alliance triumphed because it stood for freedom and peace, a cause more powerful than any starfleet. But with the New Republic decapitated and in ruins, that philosophy faces a brutal test. Before the galaxy can respond to its attack on Hosnian Prime, the First Order plans to hunt down and destroy Organa and the Resistance leaders.

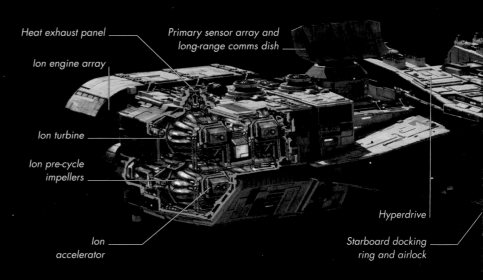

Heat exhaust panel

Primary sensor array and long-range comms dish

Ion engine array

Ion turbine

Ion pre-cycle impellers

Ion accelerator

Hyperdrive

Starboard docking ring and airlock

THE *NINKA*

The Virgillian Free Alignment was an early ally of the Rebellion, fighting a bitter civil war with its star system's Imperial-backed government. After Virgillia threw off its shackles, it became one of the Resistance's strongest supporters in the New Republic. The *Ninka*, Vice Admiral Holdo's command, is a Virgillian "Bunkerbuster" designed to carry heavy weapons and ordnance for eliminating hardened ground targets. Holdo adores her rugged little ship, but transfers her flag to the *Raddus* after taking over leadership of the fleet from an incapacitated General Organa.

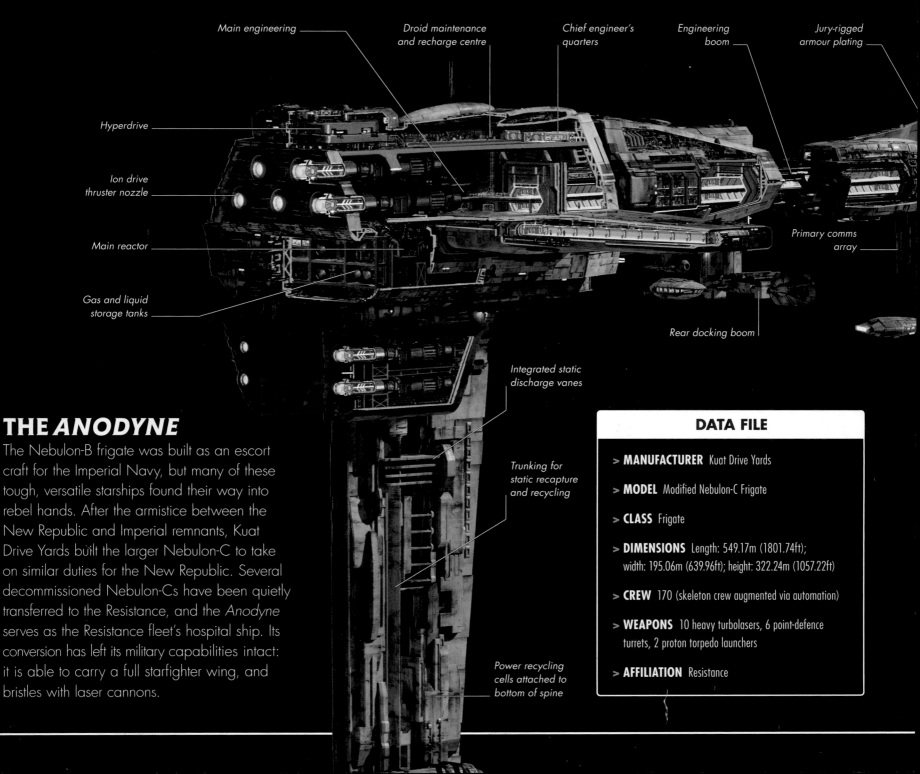

Main engineering

Droid maintenance and recharge centre

Chief engineer's quarters

Engineering boom

Jury-rigged armour plating

Hyperdrive

Ion drive thruster nozzle

Main reactor

Gas and liquid storage tanks

Primary comms array

Rear docking boom

Integrated static discharge vanes

Trunking for static recapture and recycling

Power recycling cells attached to bottom of spine

THE *ANODYNE*

The Nebulon-B frigate was built as an escort craft for the Imperial Navy, but many of these tough, versatile starships found their way into rebel hands. After the armistice between the New Republic and Imperial remnants, Kuat Drive Yards built the larger Nebulon-C to take on similar duties for the New Republic. Several decommissioned Nebulon-Cs have been quietly transferred to the Resistance, and the *Anodyne* serves as the Resistance fleet's hospital ship. Its conversion has left its military capabilities intact: it is able to carry a full starfighter wing, and bristles with laser cannons.

DATA FILE

> **MANUFACTURER** Kuat Drive Yards

> **MODEL** Modified Nebulon-C Frigate

> **CLASS** Frigate

> **DIMENSIONS** Length: 549.17m (1801.74ft); width: 195.06m (639.96ft); height: 322.24m (1057.22ft)

> **CREW** 170 (skeleton crew augmented via automation)

> **WEAPONS** 10 heavy turbolasers, 6 point-defence turrets, 2 proton torpedo launchers

> **AFFILIATION** Resistance

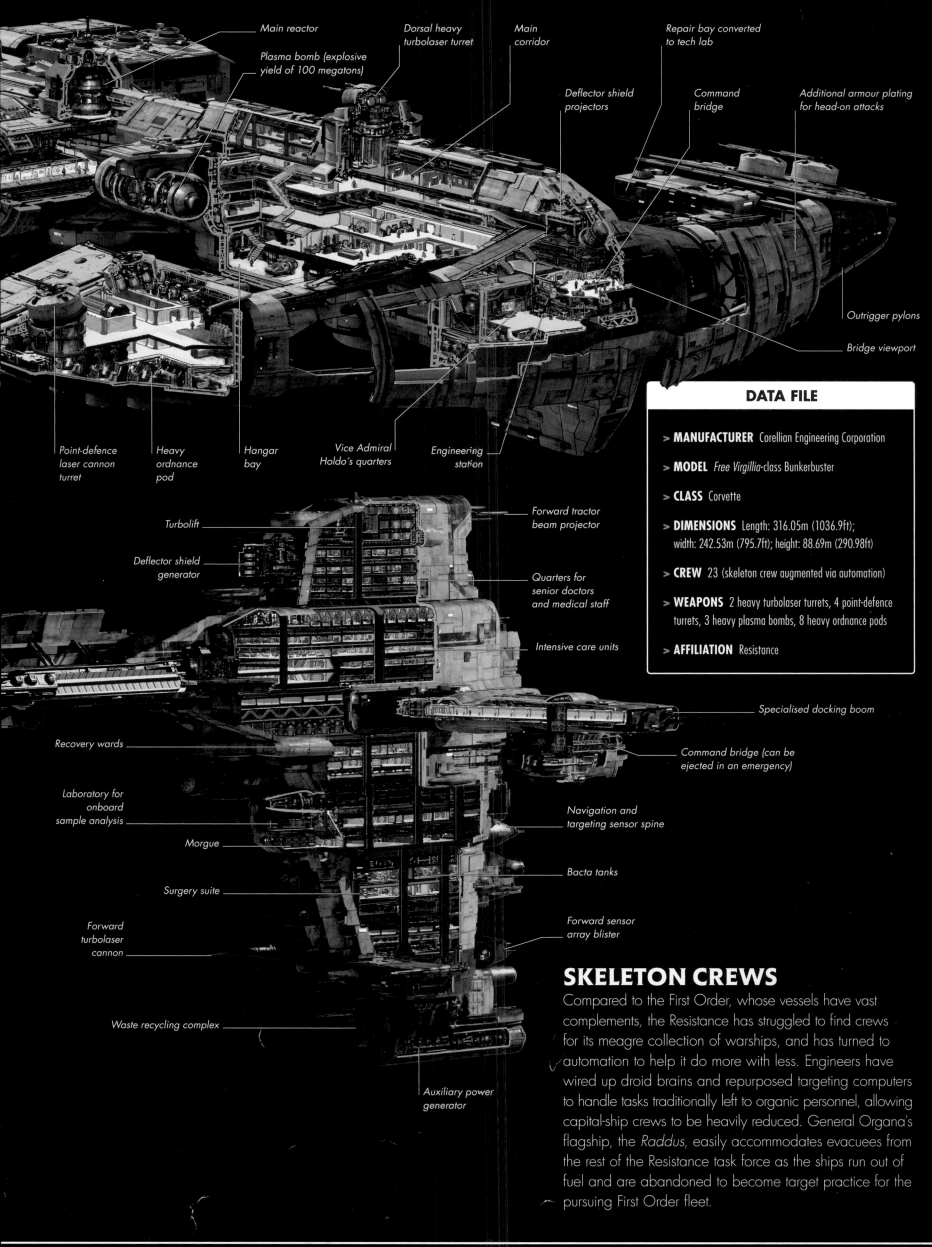

Main reactor

Dorsal heavy turbolaser turret

Main corridor

Repair bay converted to tech lab

Plasma bomb (explosive yield of 100 megatons)

Deflector shield projectors

Command bridge

Additional armour plating for head-on attacks

Outrigger pylons

Bridge viewport

Point-defence laser cannon turret

Heavy ordnance pod

Hangar bay

Vice Admiral Holdo's quarters

Engineering station

Turbolift

Forward tractor beam projector

Deflector shield generator

Quarters for senior doctors and medical staff

Intensive care units

Recovery wards

Specialised docking boom

Command bridge (can be ejected in an emergency)

Laboratory for onboard sample analysis

Navigation and targeting sensor spine

Morgue

Bacta tanks

Surgery suite

Forward turbolaser cannon

Forward sensor array blister

Waste recycling complex

Auxiliary power generator

DATA FILE

> **MANUFACTURER** Corellian Engineering Corporation

> **MODEL** *Free Virgillia*-class Bunkerbuster

> **CLASS** Corvette

> **DIMENSIONS** Length: 316.05m (1036.9ft); width: 242.53m (795.7ft); height: 88.69m (290.98ft)

> **CREW** 23 (skeleton crew augmented via automation)

> **WEAPONS** 2 heavy turbolaser turrets, 4 point-defence turrets, 3 heavy plasma bombs, 8 heavy ordnance pods

> **AFFILIATION** Resistance

SKELETON CREWS

Compared to the First Order, whose vessels have vast complements, the Resistance has struggled to find crews for its meagre collection of warships, and has turned to automation to help it do more with less. Engineers have wired up droid brains and repurposed targeting computers to handle tasks traditionally left to organic personnel, allowing capital-ship crews to be heavily reduced. General Organa's flagship, the *Raddus*, easily accommodates evacuees from the rest of the Resistance task force as the ships run out of fuel and are abandoned to become target practice for the pursuing First Order fleet.

RESISTANCE BOMBER

FLEXIBLE FLIER

PRESSING ITS WAR with the Empire's remnants, the New Republic contracted with Slayn & Korpil for the MG-100 StarFortress, a dedicated bomber that could deliver a far larger payload than starfighters. The Senate's subsequent demilitarisation effort sent many of these bombers to the scrapyard, and some found their way into Resistance hands. A mercy mission to Atterra by D'Qar's Cobalt and Crimson Squadrons left the bombers unavailable for the assault on Starkiller Base, but the squadrons' survivors arrive in time to play a pivotal role in defending D'Qar from the First Order's assault. The brave crews' sacrifice allows Resistance leaders, including General Organa and Admiral Ackbar, to evacuate their besieged headquarters.

Strapped for resources, the Resistance has improvised by using its StarFortresses on non-military missions. In the Atterra campaign, bombers delivered probes to spy on the First Order and ferried supplies to Atterra Bravo, eluding detection through powerbaffling technology that hides energy emissions. Decommissioned MG-100s also see widespread civilian use. Mining companies use them to drop explosives that break up ice and rock; local governments deploy them as rescue ships, fuel tankers and fire-fighting craft; and scout services rely on them for celestial mapping and exploration.

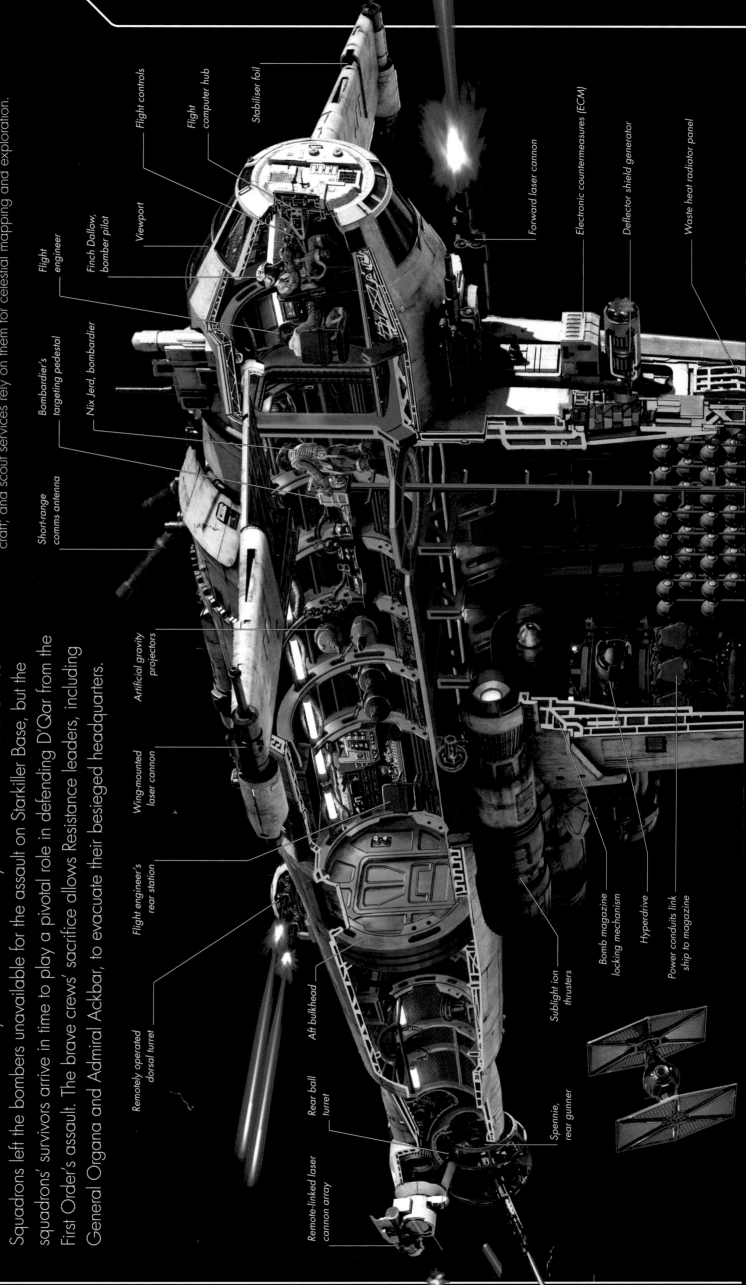

- Flight controls
- Flight computer hub
- Stabiliser foil
- Electronic countermeasures (ECM)
- Deflector shield generator
- Waste heat radiator panel
- Forward laser cannon
- Viewport
- Finch Dallow, bomber pilot
- Flight engineer
- Bombardier's targeting pedestal
- Nix Jerd, bombardier
- Short-range comms antenna
- Artificial gravity projectors
- Wing-mounted laser cannon
- Flight engineer's rear station
- Sublight ion thrusters
- Bomb magazine locking mechanism
- Hyperdrive
- Power conduits link ship to magazine
- Remotely operated dorsal turret
- Spennie, rear gunner
- Rear ball turret
- Aft bulkhead
- Remote-linked laser cannon array

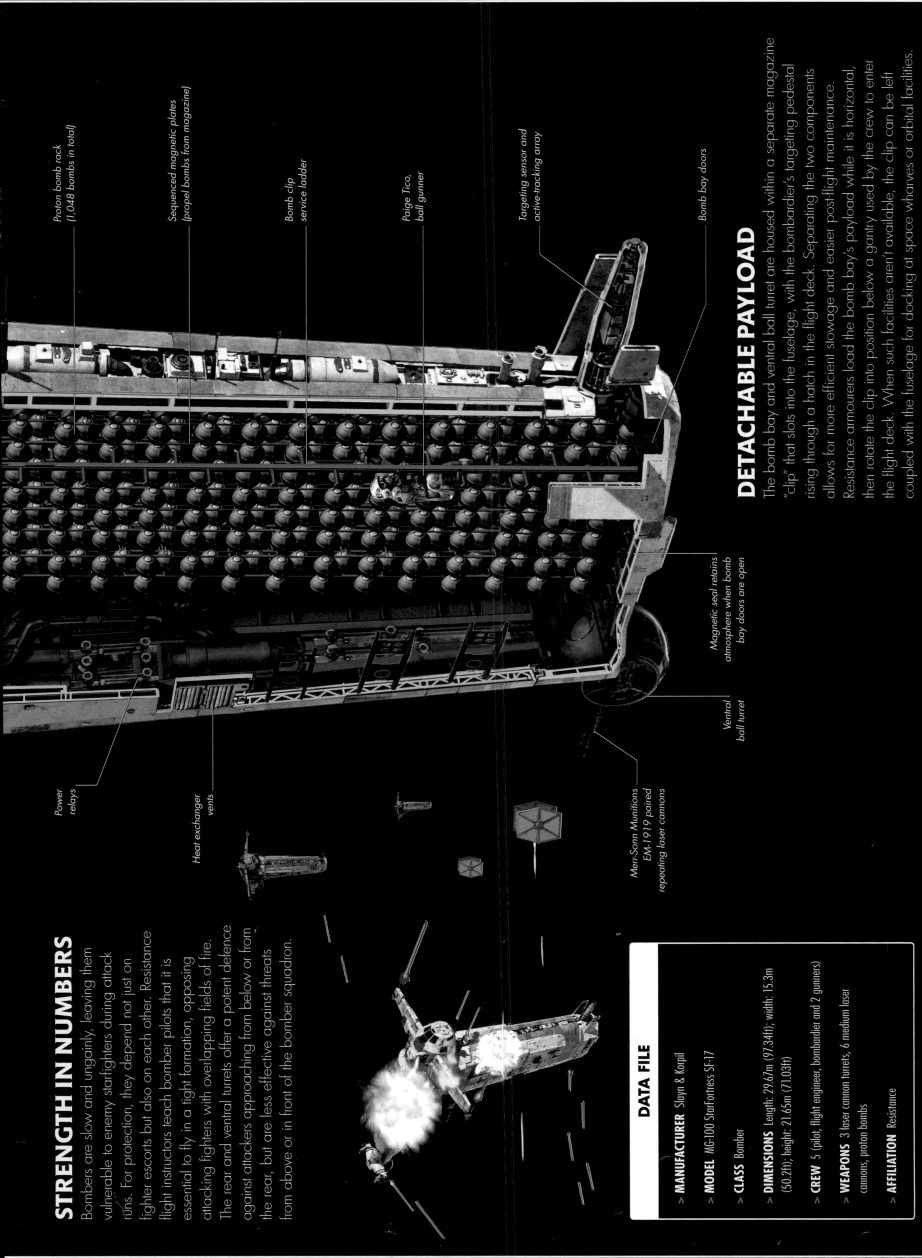

STRENGTH IN NUMBERS

Bombers are slow and ungainly, leaving them vulnerable to enemy starfighters during attack runs. For protection, they depend not just on fighter escorts but also on each other. Resistance flight instructors teach bomber pilots that it is essential to fly in a tight formation, opposing attacking fighters with overlapping fields of fire. The rear and ventral turrets offer a potent defence against attackers approaching from below or from the rear, but are less effective against threats from above or in front of the bomber squadron.

DATA FILE

> **MANUFACTURER** Slayn & Korpil

> **MODEL** MG-100 StarFortress SF-17

> **CLASS** Bomber

> **DIMENSIONS** Length: 29.67m (97.34ft); width: 15.3m (50.2ft); height: 21.65m (71.03ft)

> **CREW** 5 (pilot, flight engineer, bombardier and 2 gunners)

> **WEAPONS** 3 laser cannon turrets, 6 medium laser cannons, proton bombs

> **AFFILIATION** Resistance

DETACHABLE PAYLOAD

The bomb bay and ventral ball turret are housed within a separate magazine "clip" that slots into the fuselage, with the bombardier's targeting pedestal rising through a hatch in the flight deck. Separating the two components allows for more efficient stowage and easier post-flight maintenance. Resistance armourers load the bomb bay's payload while it is horizontal, then rotate the clip into position below a gantry used by the crew to enter the flight deck. When such facilities aren't available, the clip can be left coupled with the fuselage for docking at space wharves or orbital facilities.

Proton bomb rack
(1,048 bombs in total)

Sequenced magnetic plates
(propel bombs from magazine)

Bomb clip
service ladder

Paige Tico,
ball gunner

Targeting sensor and
active-tracking array

Bomb bay doors

Power
relays

Heat exchanger
vents

Magnetic seal retains
atmosphere when bomb
bay doors are open

Ventral
ball turret

Merr-Sonn Munitions
EM-1919 paired
repeating laser cannons

A-WING

THE SUCCESSOR to an Alliance starfighter beloved for its speed but bemoaned for frequent breakdowns, the Resistance A-wing incorporates generations of improvements by rebel techs into a sleeker, longer frame delivering stability as well as speed. The New Republic has cut A-wing production to a minimum, but the Resistance uses these fighters for everything from reconnaissance patrols to bomber escort missions. As with a previous generation's rebels, Resistance pilots take pride in proving they have the skills and daring to master this ultra-fast, yet temperamental, starfighter.

SPEED AND STEALTH

Like its rebel predecessor, the Resistance A-wing is ideal for missions that require speed: hit-and-run raids, surgical strikes on capital ships and intelligence-gathering missions. A capable pilot can emerge from hyperspace, engage the fighter's powerful suite of imagers and sensors, streak around an objective at top speed and vanish back into hyperspace, all while enemy ground crews are still scrambling to get fighters airborne. The RZ-2 improves on its predecessors' capabilities, with more powerful sensors for faster data collection and upgraded jammers to impede detection.

FIGHTER'S FOREBEARS

Kuat designers developed the original R-22 prototype as a replacement for the Republic's *Aethersprite* starfighter, but sold the initial batch to the planet Tammuz-an after the Empire rejected mass production of the craft. Rebel cells acquired several R-22s and stripped them down to boost the fighter's speed and acceleration in an effort to counter the Empire's new TIE interceptors. After these so-called RZ-1s played a key role in the Alliance's victory at Endor, Kuat resurrected its forgotten prototype to create the RZ-2, standardising years of field modifications and making the chassis slimmer and longer to yield even more speed.

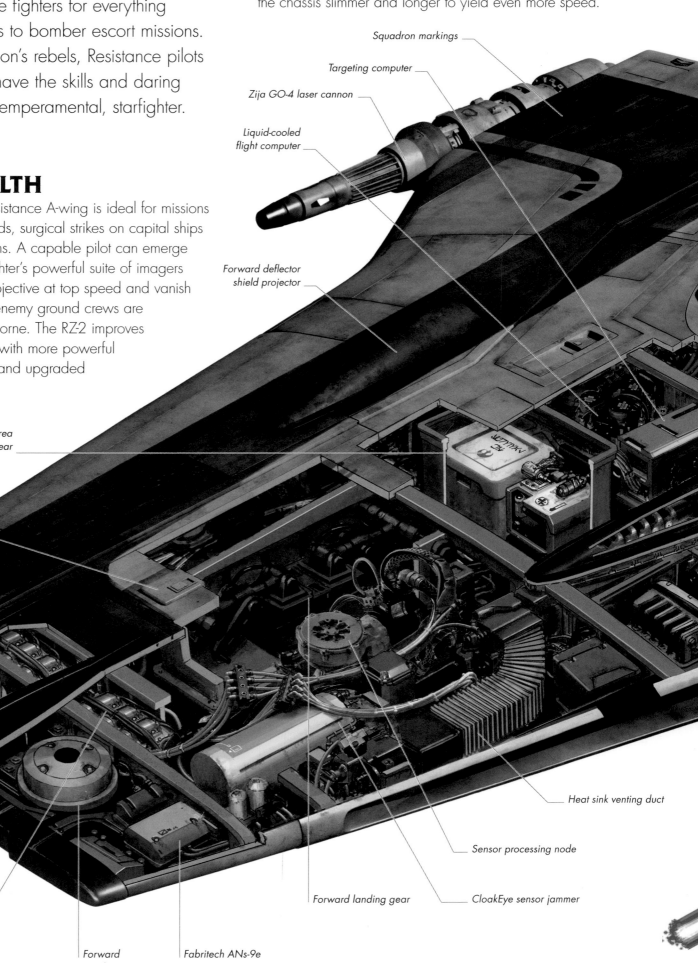

Squadron markings

Targeting computer

Zija GO-4 laser cannon

Liquid-cooled flight computer

Forward deflector shield projector

Cargo storage area contains survival gear

Maintenance diagnostic port

Towing slot used to manoeuvre craft in hangar or on the ground

Navigation sensors

Forward repulsors

Fabritech ANs-9e targeting sensor array

Forward landing gear

CloakEye sensor jammer

Sensor processing node

Heat sink venting duct

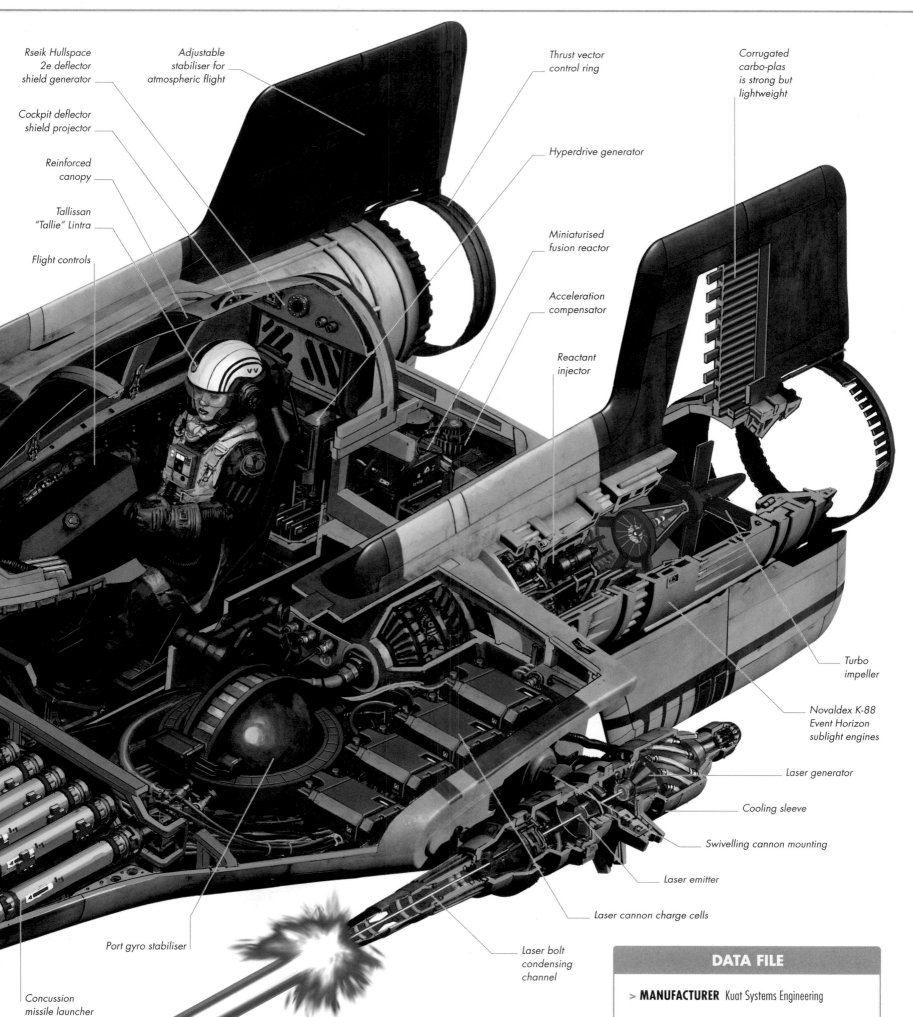

Rseik Hullspace
2e deflector
shield generator

Adjustable
stabiliser for
atmospheric flight

Thrust vector
control ring

Corrugated
carbo-plas
is strong but
lightweight

Cockpit deflector
shield projector

Hyperdrive generator

Reinforced
canopy

Miniaturised
fusion reactor

Tallissan
"Tallie" Lintra

Acceleration
compensator

Flight controls

Reactant
injector

Turbo
impeller

Novaldex K-88
Event Horizon
sublight engines

Laser generator

Cooling sleeve

Swivelling cannon mounting

Laser emitter

Laser cannon charge cells

Port gyro stabiliser

Laser bolt
condensing
channel

Concussion
missile launcher

A NEW PROFILE

By streamlining the A-wing chassis, Kuat not only delivered
more speed but also made the starfighter's notoriously
sensitive control system slightly more forgiving in flight.
Another welcome change: redesigned swivel mounts for
the laser cannons allow pilots to target enemies behind
them without worrying that the finicky mounts will jam
in that position – a chronic problem that crippled many
rebel A-wings until a return to base for maintenance.

RESISTANCE CRAFT

THE STARFIGHTER PILOTS who serve in the Resistance have no time to celebrate their victory at Starkiller Base. A First Order task force tracks them to D'Qar, determined to avenge the destruction of their planet-killing weapon by wiping out the group that has plagued them for so long. The Battle for Starkiller Base inflicted fearful losses on the Resistance's pilot ranks, forcing Poe Dameron to reform Red and Blue Squadrons with help from newly arrived A-wings and X-wings. The pilots face an immediate test – despite a shortage of fuel, they must protect bombers against waves of First Order TIEs.

DATA FILE

> **MANUFACTURER** Incom-FreiTek

> **MODEL** T-70 X-wing (modified)

> **CLASS** Starfighter

> **DIMENSIONS** Length: 12.74m (41.8ft); width: 10.81m (35.47ft); height: 4.06m (13.32ft)

> **CREW** 1 pilot plus 1 astromech droid

> **WEAPONS** 4 laser cannons, 8 proton torpedoes (standard configuration)

> **AFFILIATION** Resistance

BLACK ONE

Faster and better-armed than the rebel era's T-65 X-wings, the T-70 forms the backbone of the Resistance's starfighter corps. Poe Dameron's customised T-70, *Black One*, returned from Starkiller Base with a bad case of carbon-scoring and dangerously frayed fire-control linkages. Poe immediately ordered that his fighter be taken into a repair bay, all too aware that the Resistance's next battle would soon begin. To give himself an edge in combat, Poe ordered that an experimental thrust accelerator pod be added to *Black One*'s propulsion system.

BB-8 struggles with in-flight repairs

Magnetic flashback suppressor

Coolant feed

Experimental accelerator pod boosts Black One's speed

Main reactor cowl

Engineering boom connects hull sections

Primary sublight drive engines

THE *VIGIL*

When Gallofree Yards went bankrupt, the Empire engineered its takeover by Kuat Drive Yards, one of the regime's most staunch backers. KDY married existing Gallofree designs with elements of its Nebulon frigate line to create a series of cargo frigates, complementing cargo capacity with basic defences against pirates. The resulting ships, dubbed the *Vakbeor*-class, fared poorly, and many of them were dumped on the secondary market where, ironically, they became a favourite craft of pirate bands. Resistance commandos captured the *Vigil* from pirates in a battle off the Chasidron Shoals.

ARMOURED GUARDIANS

Within his throne room on board the *Supremacy*, Snoke's Praetorian Guard are his final line of defence. These sinister, silent warriors mercilessly cut down any who threaten their master.

THE *SUPREMACY*

A GIGANTIC WARSHIP built on an unprecedented scale, the Mega-Destroyer *Supremacy* serves Supreme Leader Snoke as both throne room and mobile command centre. Measuring more than 60 kilometres from wingtip to wingtip, this vast flying wing boasts the destructive power of a full fleet, has the industrial capability of a planet and serves as a testbed for the First Order's newest military advances. From his sanctuary deep within the *Supremacy*, Snoke ponders the fate of the galaxy and the ripples in the awakened Force – and plots the dissolution of the New Republic, the destruction of the Resistance and the downfall of the Jedi. The *Supremacy* was built at staggering cost at a secret birthplace in the Unknown Regions. With the First Order's day of destiny at hand, Snoke is finally ready to reveal it to the galaxy he intends to conquer.

The Supremacy is able to dock eight Star Destroyers at once – six externally and two internally

A HUNTER'S SECRETS

The First Order tracks targets through hyperspace using a combination of technological advances and brute-force data crunching. The shipboard tracking control complex boasts the data-sifting power of a planetary intel hub, linking huge computer arrays to databanks loaded with centuries of combat reports and astrogation data. A static hyperspace field generated around the machines then accelerates their processing power to unheard-of levels. A target's last known trajectory yields trillions of potential destinations, but the system can assess them with terrifying speed.

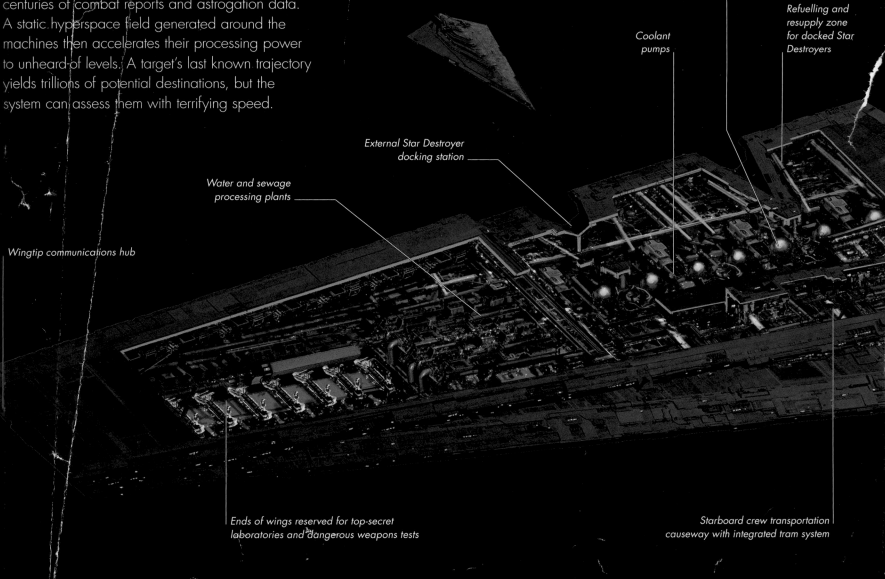

Coolant silo

Refuelling and resupply zone for docked Star Destroyers

Coolant pumps

External Star Destroyer docking station

Water and sewage processing plants

Wingtip communications hub

Ends of wings reserved for top-secret laboratories and dangerous weapons tests

Starboard crew transportation causeway with integrated tram system

INDUSTRIAL CENTRE

The *Supremacy* is the First Order's most devastating war machine and de facto headquarters. But it is also one of the regime's premier factories and research labs, with industrial capabilities that rival those of the most productive First Order worlds. Within the *Supremacy*'s armoured decks are departments reserved for conceiving, researching and approving new weapons and technology, well-stocked raw materials reserves, durasteel foundries, and state-of-the-art production lines, as well as training centres where young cadets are indoctrinated. The *Supremacy* can't be cut off from supply lines because it carries them on board.

Star Destroyer Harbinger

Detention block and interrogation rooms

Laundry room #346

Starboard #5 and #6 fusion reactor complex

Reactant silos

Multiple reactors increase redundancy and damage resistance

Hyperdrive generators

Turbolasers line surface trenches

Deflector shield projector plates

Sustenance production plant

Droid tram carries raw materials, supplies and consumables

Ground vehicle manufacturing zones

DATA FILE

> **MANUFACTURER** Slayn & Korpil

> **MODEL** Customised light shuttle

> **CLASS** Transport

> **DIMENSIONS** Length: 7.73m (25.36ft); width: 5.29m (17.36ft); height: 5.72m (18.77ft)

> **CREW** 1 pilot plus 1 passenger

> **WEAPONS** None

> **AFFILIATION** Resistance

Stabiliser fin
for atmospheric
flight

RESISTANCE TRANSPORT POD

Needing a transport capable of carrying troops and officers, Resistance techs grafted B-wing Mark II cockpits to civilian passenger modules to create a custom design. When the passenger module is detached, the cockpit section itself can be modified with a hyperdrive to serve as a light shuttle. This small, unarmed craft proves ideal for Rose and Finn to use on their rogue mission to Cantonica.

Attachment
point for
passenger
module

Pilot escape hatch/
port docking hatch

Sensor array

Cockpit seats two

Thrust vectrals
direct plasma flow

Laser turret

Command
bridge

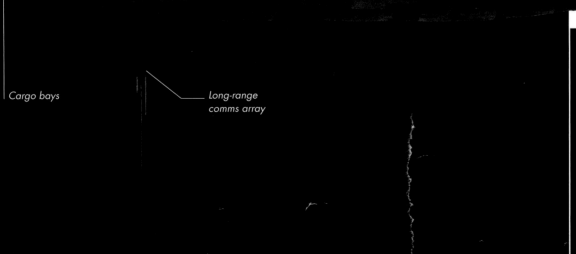

Cargo bays

Long-range
comms array

DATA FILE

> **MANUFACTURER** Kuat Drive Yards

> **MODEL** *Vakbeor*-class cargo frigate

> **CLASS** Frigate

> **DIMENSIONS** Length: 496.92m (1630.31ft); width: 79.88m (262.07ft); height: 154.46m (506.76ft)

> **CREW** 26

> **WEAPONS** 4 laser cannons, 2 tractor beam projectors

> **AFFILIATION** Resistance

Droid manufacturing plant P-3 – achieved top rank in competition with seven other shipboard facilities

Training centre for stormtrooper cadets

Quadanium armour plating

Superstructure hull bracing

Military staging areas – each can accommodate a full corps of more than 36,000 troopers

Medical centre for military staging areas

Asteroid mining complex can harvest raw materials directly from asteroid fields

SHIP OF LEGENDS

Superlatives are dangerous in a galaxy that has seen civilisations rise and fall over millennia, but the *Supremacy* may be the largest warship ever built. It dwarfs the Super Star Destroyers used by the Empire as command ships, the trophy battlecruisers built by wealthy Core sectors during the Republic's death throes and the most outlandish reconstructions of Xim the Despot's flagship. The *Supremacy*'s only rivals are the Death Star superweapons and the planetary-scaled engineering project that created Starkiller Base.

Like Supreme Leader Snoke, Kylo Ren uses the *Supremacy* as his main base of operations and safe haven. After his defeat by Rey on Starkiller Base, Kylo returns to his quarters on the flagship to heal from his injuries and plan his next move on the path to power.

MOBILE CAPITAL

Despite entreaties from commanders and allies alike, Supreme Leader Snoke has refused to designate a world as his regime's capital, either in the sectors claimed by the First Order or the Unknown Regions. The First Order's future is not to dominate a lonely corner of the Outer Rim or rule worlds beyond the galactic frontier, but to restore the Empire's stolen domain and build upon its triumphs. Until that goal is achieved, the regime's capital will travel with its master.

DATA FILE

> **MANUFACTURER** Kuat-Entralla Engineering

> **MODEL** *Mega*-class Star Dreadnought

> **CLASS** Star Dreadnought

> **DIMENSIONS** Length: 13,239.68m (43,437.27ft); width: 60,542.68m (198,630.84ft); height: 3,975.35m (13,042.49ft)

> **CREW** 2,225,000 personnel including officers, stormtroopers, gunners, vehicle engineers, factory workers, technical specialists and communications staff

> **WEAPONS** Thousands of heavy turbolasers, anti-ship missile batteries, heavy ion cannons and tractor beam projectors

> **AFFILIATION** First Order

Overbridge

Tracking
sensor nodes

Snoke's throne room

Hyperspace
tracking complex

Commons
area

Assembly hall has
seating for 200,000

Main engine
thrust nozzle

Sublight engine array – improves on
propulsion system designed for Death Stars

Manoeuvring
thrusters

Capital ship component
manufacturing

Star Destroyer
construction and
maintenance facility

Star Destroyer
enters through
ship's underside

Durasteel foundry
(one of eight)

Heavy turbolaser
tower

Droid repair
shop A16-523

Starfighter
assembly line

Water tanks

Central "city" blocks contains
majority of crew quarters

Tractor beam
projectors along
front of wing

Prow communications
nodule and integrated
sensor suite

UNPRECEDENTED SCALE

The appearance of the *Supremacy* on Resistance scopes is a
revelation far worse than anything Leia Organa had imagined.
Resistance personnel have obsessively catalogued any reported
sightings of First Order capital ships, and investigated underworld
rumours of "Snoke's boudoir". But not even the most pessimistic
member of the general's staff thought the Supreme Leader's flagship
would be on a scale to rival the now-vanquished Starkiller Base.

Star Destroyer
Conqueror

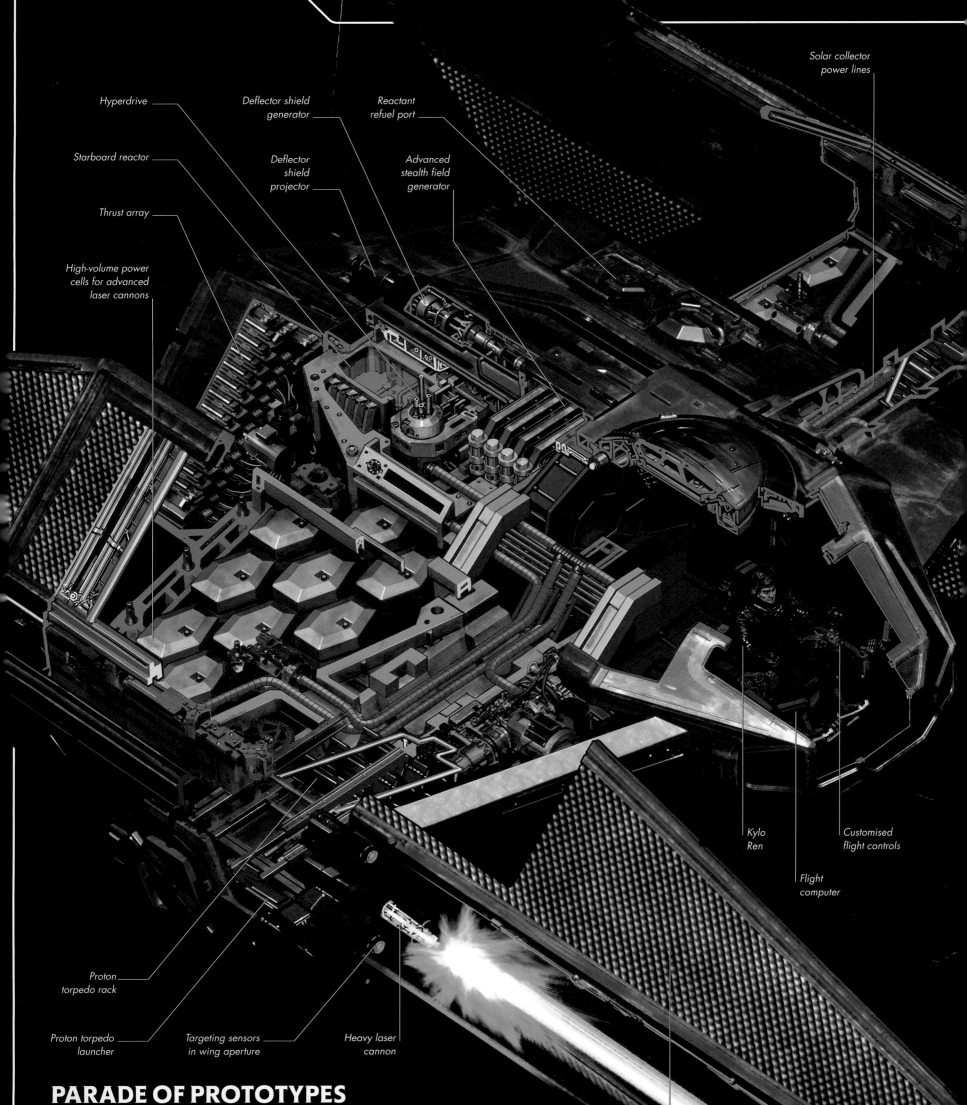

Hyperdrive

Deflector shield
generator

Reactant
refuel port

Solar collector
power lines

Starboard reactor

Deflector
shield
projector

Advanced
stealth field
generator

Thrust array

High-volume power
cells for advanced
laser cannons

Kylo
Ren

Customised
flight controls

Flight
computer

Proton
torpedo rack

Proton torpedo
launcher

Targeting sensors
in wing aperture

Heavy laser
cannon

Solar collector
array

PARADE OF PROTOTYPES

Like the Empire before it, the First Order uses prototypes to drive starfighter
development. The pedigree of the TIE silencer can be traced back to the Empire's
TIE defender, a hybrid fighter-bomber that never saw widespread use in the Galactic
Civil War, but was revived by First Order tacticians who saw it as a versatile attack
craft to throw at New Republic forces. The Special Forces TIE was an early attempt
to bring heavier weapons to the battlefield along with the next-generation power
capabilities needed to support them – improvements now incorporated in the silencer.

TIE SILENCER

AS THE FIRST ORDER closes in on the Resistance fleet, Kylo Ren leads the attack in a prototype starfighter, the TIE silencer. With a hull as black as space, the silencer is a fearsome opponent – fast enough to engage rival fighters, yet packing heavy weapons that can crack the shields and armour of capital ships. The starfighter incorporates the latest First Order military innovations, and includes experimental stealth gear meant to foil sensors and tracking. Kylo's detailed post-flight reports allow Sienar-Jaemus techs to refine onboard systems, with an eye towards the day when shipyards begin mass-producing silencers for the regime's frontline units.

DATA FILE

> **MANUFACTURER** Sienar-Jaemus Fleet Systems

> **MODEL** TIE/vn space superiority fighter

> **CLASS** Starfighter

> **DIMENSIONS** Length: 17.43m (57.19ft); width: 7.62m (25ft); height: 3.76m (12.34ft)

> **CREW** 1 pilot

> **WEAPONS** 2 Sienar-Jaemus Fleet Systems L-s9.6 laser cannons, 2 SJFS L-7.5 heavy laser cannons, Arakyd ST7 concussion and mag-pulse warhead launchers

> **AFFILIATION** First Order

Laser bolt: highly energised plasma contained in magnetic field bubble

TWIN TRADITIONS

By flying the TIE silencer against the First Order's enemies, Kylo Ren continues two traditions. Firstly, that of prototype starfighters being tested by aces, with Kylo following in the footsteps of notable Imperials such as Vult Skerris and Darth Vader. Secondly, as the son of Han Solo and grandson of Anakin Skywalker, the former Ben Solo is a natural in the cockpit.

Corrugated surface maximises energy absorption

Solar energy accumulator lines

Heat exchange matrix

Cabin access hatch

Twin ion thrust arrays

DEADLY IMPROVEMENTS

Working at hidden Sienar-Jaemus facilities, First Order designers reconfigured the weapons package of the Special Forces TIE to incorporate advances in power storage and energy conversion. The TIE/sf's power cell spokes have been replaced by a next-generation array protected beneath the hull, with shorter runs for trunk lines and converter coils. Rather than replicate the TIE/sf's ventral turret, the silencer relocates missiles and heavy cannons to the wing apertures, giving the pilot superior targeting and a wider field of fire.

FIRST ORDER CRAFT

THE ACCORDS that governed relations between the New Republic and the First Order placed strict limits on the size and capabilities of capital ships, agreements that were hailed as promises of peace for a war-weary galaxy. The D'Qar assault reveals those promises were empty: the First Order Star Destroyer *Finalizer* leads the attack, accompanied by a huge Siege Dreadnought. More than two dozen other Star Destroyers then join the fight, accompanied by the First Order's mightiest warship – Snoke's aptly named Mega-Destroyer, the *Supremacy*.

Advanced sensor suites scan for enemies

Wings extend and retract along guide rails

Passenger compartment sits aft of cockpit

DATA FILE

> **MANUFACTURER** Sienar-Jaemus Fleet Systems

> **MODEL** *Upsilon*-class command shuttle

> **CLASS** Transport

> **DIMENSIONS** Length: 19.19m (62.96ft); width: 13.53m (44.39ft); height: 37.2m (122.05ft)

> **CREW** 1–5 plus up to 10 passengers

> **WEAPONS** 2 twin heavy laser cannons

> **AFFILIATION** First Order

COMMAND SHUTTLE

These black, bat-winged shuttles carry First Order dignitaries such as Kylo Ren. Communications monitors, scanning suites, shield projectors and powerful jammers line their tall, extendable wings, protecting the shuttles' valuable passengers from attack.

Twin heavy laser cannons

Long-range sensor tower

Command bridge

Point-defence turrets cover surface

Tractor beam projectors

Orbital bombardment cannon

DATA FILE

> **MANUFACTURER** Kuat-Entralla Engineering

> **MODEL** *Mandator IV*-class Siege Dreadnought

> **CLASS** Star Dreadnought

> **DIMENSIONS** Length: 7,669.71m (25,163.09ft); width: 4,121.02m (13,520.41ft); height: 770.85m (2,529.04ft)

> **CREW** 53,000 officers, 140,000 enlisted, 22,000 stormtroopers

> **WEAPONS** 2 orbital bombardment cannons, 26 dorsal point-defence turrets, 6 tractor beam projectors

> **AFFILIATION** First Order

DREADNOUGHT

One of the First Order's largest warships, the *Fulminatrix* is a Siege Dreadnought that dwarfs General Hux's flagship, the *Finalizer*. The *Fulminatrix* is the latest in the *Mandator* line, which originated in the decades before the Clone Wars. The Dreadnought's underside holds massive orbital bombardment cannons that can punch through planetary shields, then rain destruction on enemy worlds.

LIGHT SHUTTLE

The First Order uses compact, hardy *Xi*-class light shuttles for everything from ferrying officers to transporting equipment. Unlike larger command shuttles, *Xi*-class shuttles have only light weapons and minimal shields, relying on fighter escorts for protection. Rose and Finn escape the *Supremacy* in a stolen light shuttle.

Top wing incorporates sensor jammers

Ion engine manifold

Cockpit offers excellent visibility

DATA FILE

> **MANUFACTURER** Sienar-Jaemus Fleet Systems

> **MODEL** *Xi*-class light shuttle

> **CLASS** Transport

> **DIMENSIONS** Length: 11.84m (38.84ft); width: 22.87m (75.04ft); height: 18.31m (60.08ft)

> **CREW** 1–2 plus up to 6 passengers

> **WEAPONS** 2 light laser cannons

> **AFFILIATION** First Order

Low conning tower is better protected than old Imperial designs

Command bridge

Hypermatter reactor hull chassis

STAR DESTROYER

During his mission to Jakku, Poe Dameron was held captive aboard the *Finalizer*, first of a long-rumoured new class of First Order Star Destroyers built in secret shipyards deep within the Unknown Regions. More than two dozen of these warships join the pursuit of the Resistance fleet. Besides heavy turbolasers powered by kyber crystals, each Star Destroyer carries a full legion of stormtroopers, a hundred assault craft and two starfighter wings.

DATA FILE

> **MANUFACTURER** Kuat-Entralla Engineering

> **MODEL** *Resurgent*-class Star Destroyer

> **CLASS** Battlecruiser

> **DIMENSIONS** Length: 2,915.84m (9,566.4ft); width: 1,483.5m (4,867.13ft); height: 496.89m (1,630.22ft)

> **CREW** 19,000 officers, 55,000 enlisted, 8,000 stormtroopers

> **WEAPONS** More than 1,500 turbolasers, point-defence laser cannons and ion cannons

> **AFFILIATION** First Order

TIE FIGHTERS

Like their Imperial predecessors, standard First Order TIE fighters (TIE/fo) lack hyperdrives and are limited to short-range operations, but these new-generation TIEs are defended by shields, miniaturised by years of research in First Order labs. The Special Forces TIE (TIE/sf) is a versatile attack ship that carries a gunner as well as a pilot, is outfitted with a hyperdrive and is equipped with a turret carrying more powerful weapons.

DATA FILE

> **MANUFACTURER** Sienar-Jaemus Fleet Systems

> **MODELS** TIE/fo space superiority fighter, TIE/sf space superiority fighter

> **CLASS** Starfighter

> **DIMENSIONS** Length: 6.69m (21.96ft); width 6.34m (20.8ft); height: 8.17m (26.8ft)

> **CREW** 1 pilot (TIE/fo), 1 pilot and 1 gunner (TIE/sf)

> **WEAPONS** 2 laser cannons (TIE/fo), 2 laser cannons, 1 dual heavy laser turret, 1 concussion and mag-pulse warhead launcher (TIE/sf)

> **AFFILIATION** First Order

Pre-charged power cells

TIE/SF

Heavy weapons turret

Subspace communications antenna

TIE/FO

Solar-collecting arrays feed improved power cells

CANTO BIGHT POLICE SPEEDER

CANTO BIGHT'S winding alleys and promenades are difficult terrain for the heavy speeders favoured by most police forces, so local law enforcement depends on nimble repulsorcraft known as jet-sticks. These craft are easy to control, with officers directing them by leaning one way or the other, and accelerating and braking with foot pedals and hand-held throttles. Their laser cannons are generally set for stun, but can kill a humanoid or disable a civilian vehicle at full power. While jet-sticks are not capable of true atmospheric flight, they can easily reach rooftop level or cross small stretches of water.

DATA FILE

> **MANUFACTURER** Trochiliad Motors

> **MODEL** Cantonica zephyr GB-134 jet-stick

> **CLASS** Speeder bike

> **DIMENSIONS** Length: 2.98m (9.78ft); width: 2.55m (8.37ft); height: 2.5m (8.2ft)

> **CREW** 1 police officer

> **WEAPONS** 2 anti-personnel laser cannons

> **AFFILIATION** Canto Bight Police Department

QUICK RESPONSE

The whir of a jet-stick's rotors reassures visitors to Canto Bight that the police are keeping an eye out for shady characters drawn to the glitz and glamour of galactic high life. Officers use dash-mounted data displays to identify troublemakers and exchange information while hovering in the old city's graceful squares, or patrolling the labyrinth of ancient streets. In the event of trouble, an officer activates the jet-stick's sirens and speeds to the scene, ready to coordinate with foot patrols or call for backup from heavier units.

KEEPING THE PEACE

The Canto Bight Police Department is well equipped and its officers are well paid. This is all part of Cantonica's strategy to keep the wealthy engaged at gaming tables and racetracks, so credits flow freely from their pockets and into the coffers of the planet's entertainment barons. The police are trained to avoid deadly force if at all possible, keeping Canto Bight a sunny playground free of shadows cast by inequality and galactic unrest. The CBPD uses jet-sticks to contain trouble, responding quickly, firing stun bolts and carting miscreants off to answer for their crimes at the convenience of a magistrate.

Repulsor projection grid

Repulsor field amplification node

Police light

Manoeuvring repulsors

Power dynamos

Power distribution pylon

Power converters

Repulsor field generation frame

Canto Bight Mounted
Police officer

Data display

Flight
computer
chip boards

Searchlight

Pilot controls
direction by
leaning

Rear
power cell

Primary heat
exhaust

Structural
bracing

Cooling
sleeve

Power
trunking

Static
discharge
vanes

Altitude
controls

Forward light

Canto Bight Police
Department livery

Long-range
comlink

Brake

Operator
pylon

Accelerator
pedal

Forward
power cells

Power
relays

Multi-setting
laser cannon
can be set from
stun to kill

Terrain sensor

JUMPSPEEDERS AND AIRHOOKS

Jet-sticks and other personal
repulsorlift craft have proved popular
with those who must travel regularly
within limited areas, such as police
officers and factory workers. They
also appeal to tourists exploring the
sights on exotic worlds. Personal
repulsorcraft operated while sitting
are often called jumpspeeders,
while those driven in a standing
position are known as airhooks.
An infamous airhook model was
the STAP, flown by battle droids
during the Clone Wars.

CANTO BIGHT SPEEDERS

THE ENTRANCES to Canto Bight's casinos aren't just a prelude to the pleasures waiting within, but a stage for showing off a dizzying array of luxury speeders, many of them heavily customised by the mod shops in Canto Bight's Old Town. Well-connected visitors reserve flashy rides before their arrival, with chauffeurs available for those who'd rather be driven than take the controls themselves. The night-time thoroughfares of Canto Bight are a parade of gleaming, growling street machines, and many a visitor leaves delighted by the display and wanting to own a piece of it. The mod shops soon find themselves with another customer boasting an outsized bank account and requesting a creation that will make even the most jaded head turn.

Gamblers arriving for a night at the tables are greeted by valets trained to operate speeders designed for a vast range of appendages. There are also droids on hand to take charge of truly exotic models. Holo-camera trackers alert staff when a visitor's night is over, ensuring minimal wait times.

Passenger cabin with low-slung windshield

Airscoop cools repulsorlift matrix

Multispectrum headlights

Cantonica waiver has declared Saltaire 9000 drive turbines street legal

Drive turbine air intake

GROWLER-556

Curious visitors who follow the whine of laser cutters into the warrens of Old Town find all-night mod shops, where speeders are transformed into powerful machines that double as works of street art. Kingby Feruil's tricked-out Growler-556 is a prowling advertisement for this trade: its twin turbines give it a flight ceiling of 50 metres, which would be illegal if not for a waiver granted after a generous donation to the Cantonica Transportation Ministry pension fund.

DATA FILE

> **MANUFACTURER** Astikan Gridworx

> **MODEL** Growler-556 (modified)

> **CLASS** Landspeeder

> **CREW** 1 pilot, 1 passenger

> **WEAPONS** None

> **AFFILIATION** None

STREETBOSS 50-50

Experience and training mean valets and chauffeurs typically park visitors' speeders with confidence. However, Hulb Toxx's vehicle is an exception, as every valet learns in short order. Hulb's StreetBoss 50-50 not only parks itself, but also defends its chosen turf with proximity alerts and an anti-personnel energy grid powerful enough to leave a Wookiee drooling and staggering. When the StreetBoss arrives, normally attentive valets blanch and scatter.

Drive turbines tucked in to ensure stylish silhouette

Chromium-alloy plating with integrated chromomites

SOLARNOVA TT-86

Thandisten Pikalo's SolarNova TT-86 is something that's rarely seen in the street parade: a completely unmodified speeder. But you don't need the services of a mod shop when you own one of six prototypes built by the artisans of Vanguerre XI, before the collective shut its doors and dissolved on the eve of the Clone Wars.

Forward hazard sensors

Kismet-1010 outrigger drive turbine

Repulsor array cowling

TRI-VANQUISH 7

As a speeder-modder himself, Si-Cos Tejujuar places bets alongside clients past, present and future. His latest creation is a custom speeder built on a SoroSuub Tri-Vanquish 7 frame, altered to carry outrigger turbines, a rakish smoked-glass windscreen and repulsorlifts that emit a resonant, subsonic purr. Canto Bight's valets know to take their time parking Teju's creations, ensuring that they catch envious visitors' notice.

THE *LIBERTINE*

FOR THE JOURNEY from Cantonica to the First Order fleet, DJ decides to travel in style, searching Canto Bight's spaceport for a ride worthy of the rich payday he is about to enjoy. For a practised criminal, it is all too easy. He slips past the guards and uses a computer spike and key bypass to slice through the anti-theft defences of the *Libertine*, a sleek and stylish star yacht belonging to a high-rolling executive turned arms dealer. The handsome yacht lacks weapons and robust defensive systems, which reflects its origins in a safer galactic era – as well as an aristocrat's certainty that wealth and breeding are safeguards against disaster and bad luck. DJ knows better; perhaps the *Libertine*'s owner will reach the same conclusion once he finds his prized yacht for sale in a black-market ship lot, stripped of its most valuable equipment and finest trappings.

STATUS SYMBOL

DJ grins at the sight of the staircase connecting the *Libertine*'s lounge with its flight deck. This seemingly out-of-place detail is a hallmark of a top-of-the-line yacht, one constructed with acceleration compensators and antishock fields to ensure a ride as smooth as a luxury airspeeder or groundcoach. Unfortunately, he'll have to ditch the yacht in short order. But that's all right – in an easy-come, easy-go galaxy, a wise being doesn't cling to possessions, but simply enjoys the ride.

Atmosphere intake vents

Chromium detailing

Communications spine

Hull plates interwoven with radiation shielding

Starboard repulsorlift manoeuvring vane

Sensor node

Emergency beacon

Highly reflective luxury hull coating

Forward deflector shield projector

SEEKING DIVERSION

The *Libertine*'s owner is Korfé Bennux-Ai, born into wealth on Celanon and a top-ranking manager for the Sienar-Jaemus corporation. Bennux-Ai has made a fortune selling starfighters that fail the First Order's stringent quality checks to nervous star systems seeking to bolster their defences. Frustrated by a failed deal with Zygerrian slavers, Bennux-Ai ordered his pilots to divert to Cantonica for a restorative night on the town.

Power relay conduits

Sensor spine

Power converter for forward systems

Overclocked forward repulsors allow for nimble micromanoeuvres

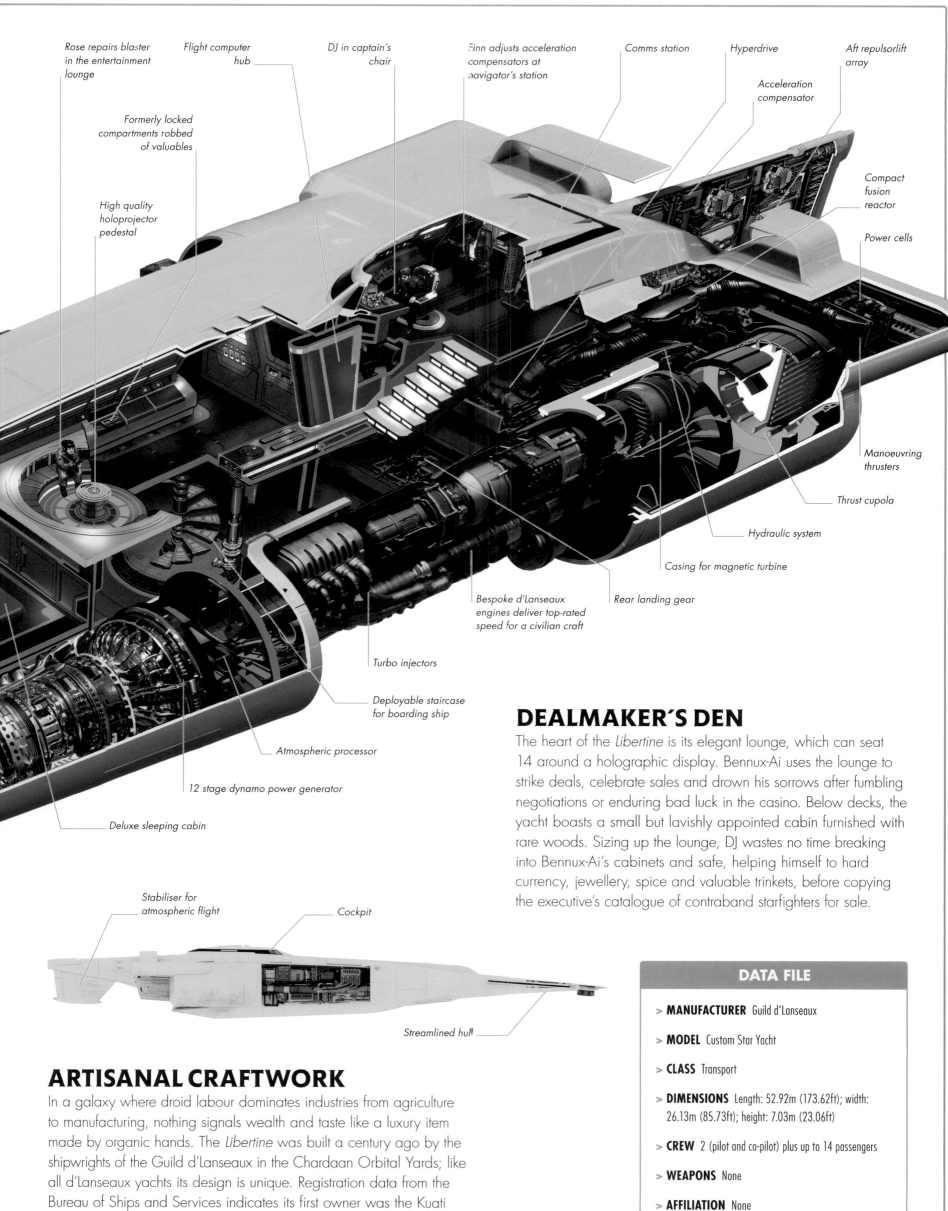

Rose repairs blaster in the entertainment lounge

Formerly locked compartments robbed of valuables

High quality holoprojector pedestal

Flight computer hub

DJ in captain's chair

Finn adjusts acceleration compensators at navigator's station

Comms station

Hyperdrive

Acceleration compensator

Aft repulsorlift array

Compact fusion reactor

Power cells

Manoeuvring thrusters

Thrust cupola

Hydraulic system

Casing for magnetic turbine

Rear landing gear

Bespoke d'Lanseaux engines deliver top-rated speed for a civilian craft

Turbo injectors

Deployable staircase for boarding ship

Atmospheric processor

12 stage dynamo power generator

Deluxe sleeping cabin

Stabiliser for atmospheric flight

Cockpit

Streamlined hull

DEALMAKER'S DEN

The heart of the *Libertine* is its elegant lounge, which can seat 14 around a holographic display. Bennux-Ai uses the lounge to strike deals, celebrate sales and drown his sorrows after fumbling negotiations or enduring bad luck in the casino. Below decks, the yacht boasts a small but lavishly appointed cabin furnished with rare woods. Sizing up the lounge, DJ wastes no time breaking into Bennux-Ai's cabinets and safe, helping himself to hard currency, jewellery, spice and valuable trinkets, before copying the executive's catalogue of contraband starfighters for sale.

ARTISANAL CRAFTWORK

In a galaxy where droid labour dominates industries from agriculture to manufacturing, nothing signals wealth and taste like a luxury item made by organic hands. The *Libertine* was built a century ago by the shipwrights of the Guild d'Lanseaux in the Chardaan Orbital Yards; like all d'Lanseaux yachts its design is unique. Registration data from the Bureau of Ships and Services indicates its first owner was the Kuati diplomat Valis of Kuhlvult, who christened the ship the *Steadfast*.

DATA FILE

> **MANUFACTURER** Guild d'Lanseaux

> **MODEL** Custom Star Yacht

> **CLASS** Transport

> **DIMENSIONS** Length: 52.92m (173.62ft); width: 26.13m (85.73ft); height: 7.03m (23.06ft)

> **CREW** 2 (pilot and co-pilot) plus up to 14 passengers

> **WEAPONS** None

> **AFFILIATION** None

AT-HH

TUG WALKERS ARE BUILT to do one job: pull incredibly heavy loads under battlefield conditions. Their rows of legs – a design reminiscent of crustaceans or insects – supply enormous power while allowing the vehicle to keep moving even if multiple limbs are lost. Formally known as All Terrain Heavy Haulers (AT-HHs), tug walkers rely on a combination of escort vehicles and heavy onboard weapons for defence. Their flat top decks are sheathed in thick armour plates, and four swivelling corner turrets can repel attackers from all sides. AT-HHs are used to drag everything from disabled warships to prefabricated base modules. However, on Crait their payload is a terrifying First Order weapon: a mighty siege cannon whose destructive power relies on kyber crystals similar to those at the heart of the Death Stars' superlasers.

STRENGTH IN NUMBERS

Traditional walkers can simply step over obstacles that would foil wheeled and tracked vehicles, but losing even a single leg can turn them into stalled scrap. The AT-HH borrows a strategy from the insect world: more legs means greater stability. The tug walker has three rows of legs; the front row holds 11 legs, while the rear two rows each have 10. The legs can rotate around their attachment points and be repositioned within the rows – in field tests on Dromondar Beta, AT-HHs were able to fulfil mission objectives with more than 40 per cent of their limbs inoperative.

INTERLOCKING DEFENCES

An obvious way to stop the siege cannon would be to disable or destroy the tugs themselves. But that's easier said than done with an AT-HH – in addition to thick armour and redundant legs, the tug walker can defend itself with the turrets mounted at each corner of its carapace. First Order tactics also call for tug walkers to be defended by escorts ranging from TIE fighters to AT-ATs, AT-M6s and troopers patrolling on speeders.

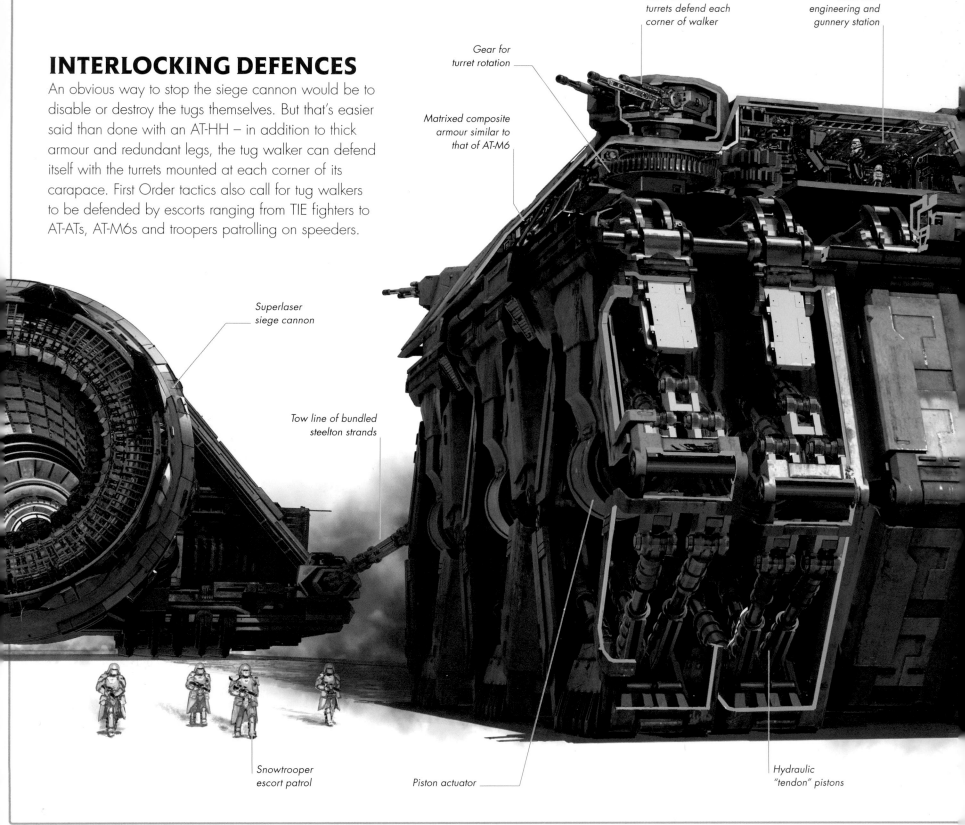

Laser cannon
turrets defend each
corner of walker

Starboard
engineering and
gunnery station

Gear for
turret rotation

Matrixed composite
armour similar to
that of AT-M6

Superlaser
siege cannon

Tow line of bundled
steelton strands

Snowtrooper
escort patrol

Piston actuator

Hydraulic
"tendon" pistons

Tow cable
observation post

> **MANUFACTURER** Kuat-Entralla Drive Yards

> **MODEL** All Terrain Heavy Hauler (AT-HH)

> **CLASS** Tug walker

> **DIMENSIONS** Length: 29.57m (97ft); width: 27.43m (89.99ft); height: 14.29m (46.88ft)

> **CREW** 9 (2 pilots, vehicle commander, 2 engineers and 4 gunners)

> **WEAPONS** 4 medium fire-linked dual laser cannons

> **AFFILIATION** First Order

Fusion reactor

Fuel cells

Heat exchanger vents

TOUGH TETHERS

To drcg the giant superlaser cannon into position, the First Order uses a method that would be recognised by ancient armies on countless worlds – tow cables. These would seem like a weak point, but as the Resistance discovers, they're anything but: each strand is actually a bundle of 27,572 steelton wires, an assemblage able to shrug off many direct hits from laser cannons before parting. The Resistance lacks both the time and the firepower to detach the AT-HHs from the deadly cannon making its way across Crait's salt flats.

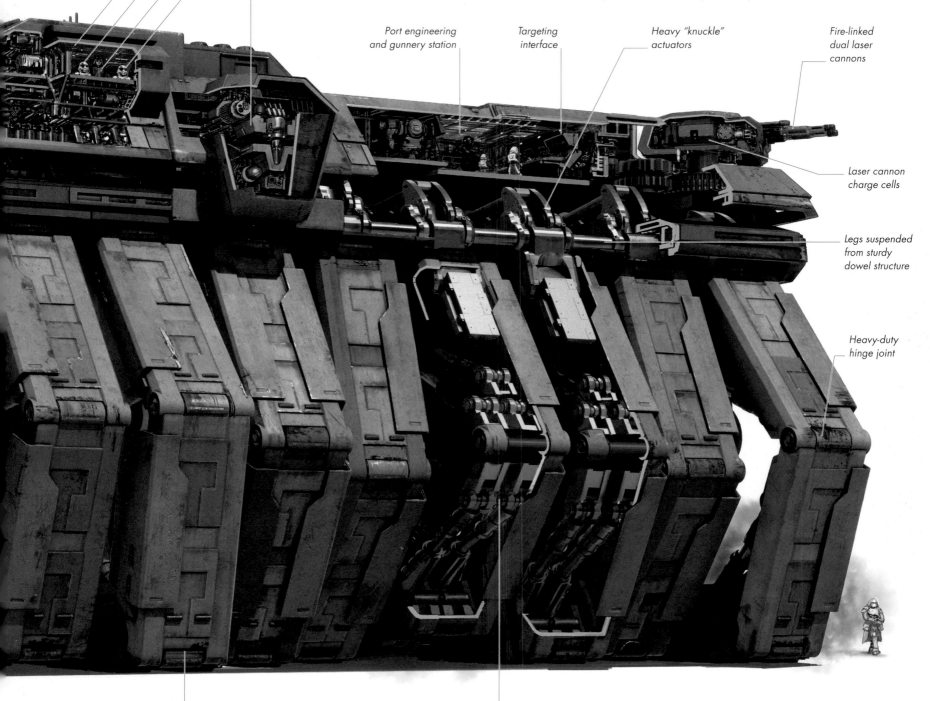

Bridge

Pilot

Commander

Co-pilot

Primary sensor node hub

Port engineering and gunnery station

Targeting interface

Heavy "knuckle" actuators

Fire-linked dual laser cannons

Laser cannon charge cells

Legs suspended from sturdy dowel structure

Heavy-duty hinge joint

Redundant legs allow walker to keep moving if damaged

Refined durasteel bearing

AT-M6

A TOWERING MACHINE seemingly plucked from nightmares, the All Terrain MegaCalibre Six brings devastating firepower to the surface of Crait. Sheathed in state-of-the-art armour forged in secret facilities in the Unknown Regions, the massive AT-M6 is simultaneously a brutally effective siege engine and a fiendish example of psychological warfare. It is a menacing symbol of an emboldened First Order that rejected its Imperial predecessors. The goal of such galaxy that rejected its Imperial predecessors. The goal of such an obscene display of murderous power is to reduce enemies to abject terror, incapable of any course of action except total submission.

TOP GUN

The AT-M6 is fundamentally a platform for the MegaCalibre Six turbolaser cannon, which dominates the walker's massive fuselage. Intended to make siege warfare simple and short, the M6 is powerful enough to punch through shields rated to deflect bombardment from orbit. Bringing the destructive power of a battleship to ground engagements requires a dedicated power plant and a string of auxiliary fuel cells to reduce the cannon's recharge time.

DATA FILE

> **MANUFACTURER** Kuat-Entralla Drive Yards

> **MODEL** All Terrain MegaCalibre Six (AT-M6)

> **CLASS** Combat walker

> **DIMENSIONS** Length: 40.87m (134.09ft); width: 17.95m (58.89ft); height: 36.18m (118.7ft)

> **CREW** 5 (pilot, gunner, vehicle commander and 2 weapon engineers) plus up to 12 passengers

> **WEAPONS** 1 MegaCalibre Six turbolaser cannon, 2 heavy fire-linked dual laser cannons, 2 medium anti-ship laser cannons

> **AFFILIATION** First Order

Heat exhaust

Gun deck access ladder

Turbolaser fuel cells

Auxiliary space can be customised depending on mission profile

Seats for small number of embarked infantry

Main fusion reactor

Reactor coil

Reactant fuel port

Weapon diagnostics interface

Weapon crew

Dedicated power plant for turbolaser

Recoil shock absorber

Targeting sensors

Main limb locomotion pistons

MegaCalibre Six turbolaser cannon

Anti-ship laser cannon

Chin-mounted heavy laser cannons

Pilot and gunnery officer stations

Vehicle commander

Fire control and targeting computer

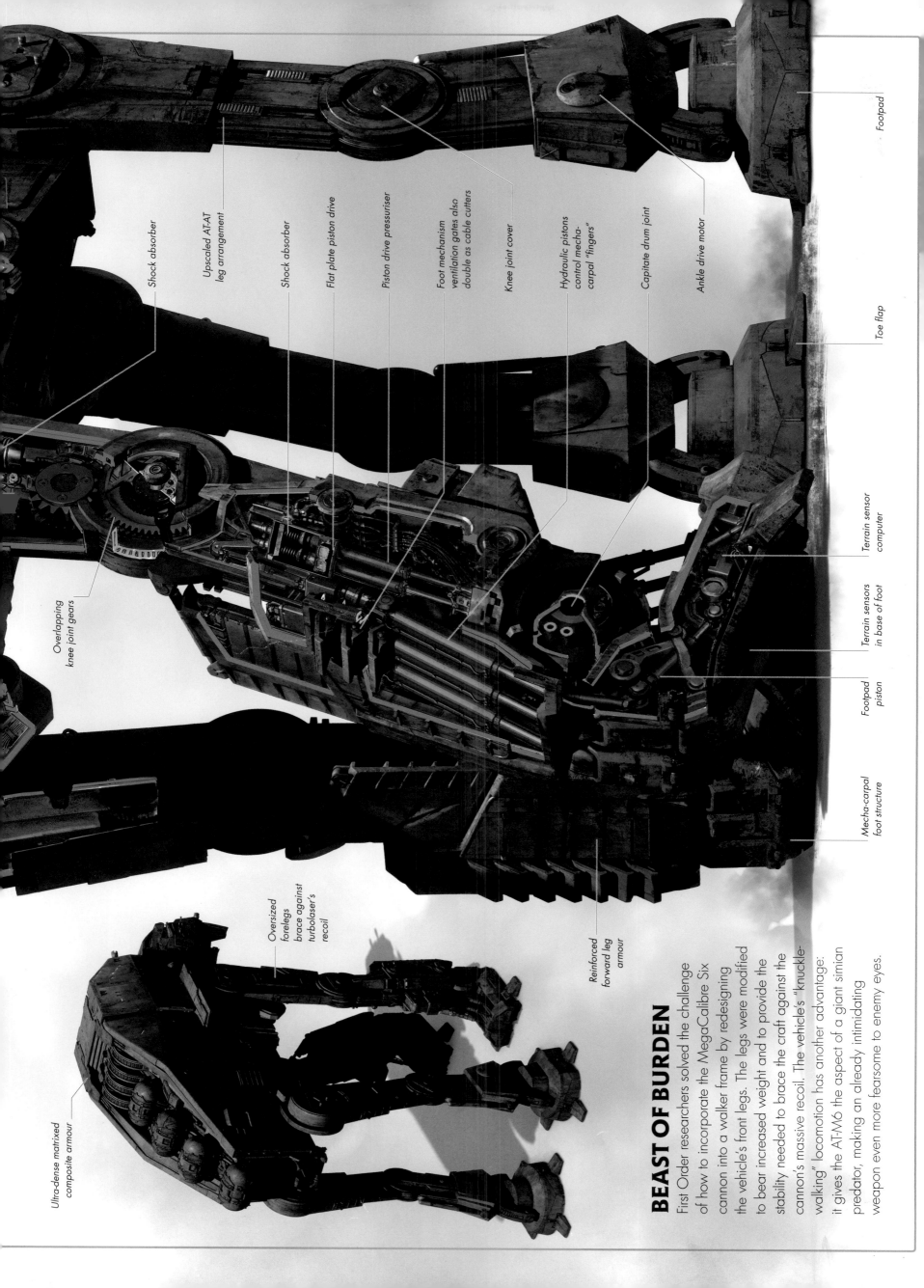

Shock absorber

Upscaled AT-AT
leg arrangement

Shock absorber

Flat plate piston drive

Piston drive pressuriser

Foot mechanism
ventilation gates also
double as cable cutters

Knee joint cover

Hydraulic pistons
control mecha-
carpal "fingers"

Capitate drum joint

Ankle drive motor

Footpad

Toe flap

Terrain sensor
computer

Terrain sensors
in base of foot

Overlapping
knee joint gears

Footpad
piston

Mecha-carpal
foot structure

Oversized
forelegs
brace against
turbolaser's
recoil

Reinforced
forward leg
armour

BEAST OF BURDEN

First Order researchers solved the challenge
of how to incorporate the MegaCalibre Six
cannon into a walker frame by redesigning
the vehicle's front legs. The legs were modified
to bear increased weight and to provide the
stability needed to brace the craft against the
cannon's massive recoil. The vehicle's "knuckle-
walking" locomotion has another advantage:
it gives the AT-M6 the aspect of a giant simian
predator, making an already intimidating
weapon even more fearsome to enemy eyes.

Ultra-dense matrixed
composite armour

FIRST ORDER WALKERS

THE FIRST ORDER planned its ascendance in hidden labs and secret shipyards beyond the veil of the galactic frontier, pursuing advances in weapons, armour and related fields that built on Imperial research to create fearsome new war machines. But First Order scientists haven't let these advances blind them to the effectiveness of designs inherited from their predecessors. The assault force carried to Crait by Snoke's fleet includes not only AT-M6s, AT-HHs and a superlaser siege cannon, but also familiar-looking AT-ATs and AT-STs.

Reinforced composite armour

Light blaster cannon

Concussion grenade launcher

Gyro mounting for cockpit traverse

Gyroscopically stabilised femoral strut

Armoured shield for knee joint

External armour plating

Rear hull contains high-density power cells

Unit marking

Internal shock-absorbing system

AT–ST

Two-legged scout walkers are useful for a range of mission profiles, from reconnaissance and support to anti-personnel search-and-destroy sweeps. Their smaller size makes them faster and more manoeuvrable than full-sized AT-ATs, enabling them to cross difficult terrain that would bring their larger cousins to a halt. The First Order's AT-STs are more stable than Imperial models thanks to improved gyroscopic systems, and are clad in next-generation armour that is lightweight but strong.

Compression gearing stabilises ankle

Shin strut

Footpad tipped with fence-cutting blade

Footpad lined with terrain sensors

DATA FILE

> **MANUFACTURER** Kuat-Entralla Drive Yards

> **MODEL** First Order All Terrain Scout Transport (AT-ST)

> **CLASS** Combat walker

> **DIMENSIONS** Length: 6.43m (21.1ft); width: 4.61m (15.12ft); height: 8.89m (29.17ft)

> **CREW** 2 (pilot and gunner)

> **WEAPONS** 1 twin blaster cannon, 1 light blaster cannon, 1 concussion grenade launcher

> **AFFILIATION** First Order

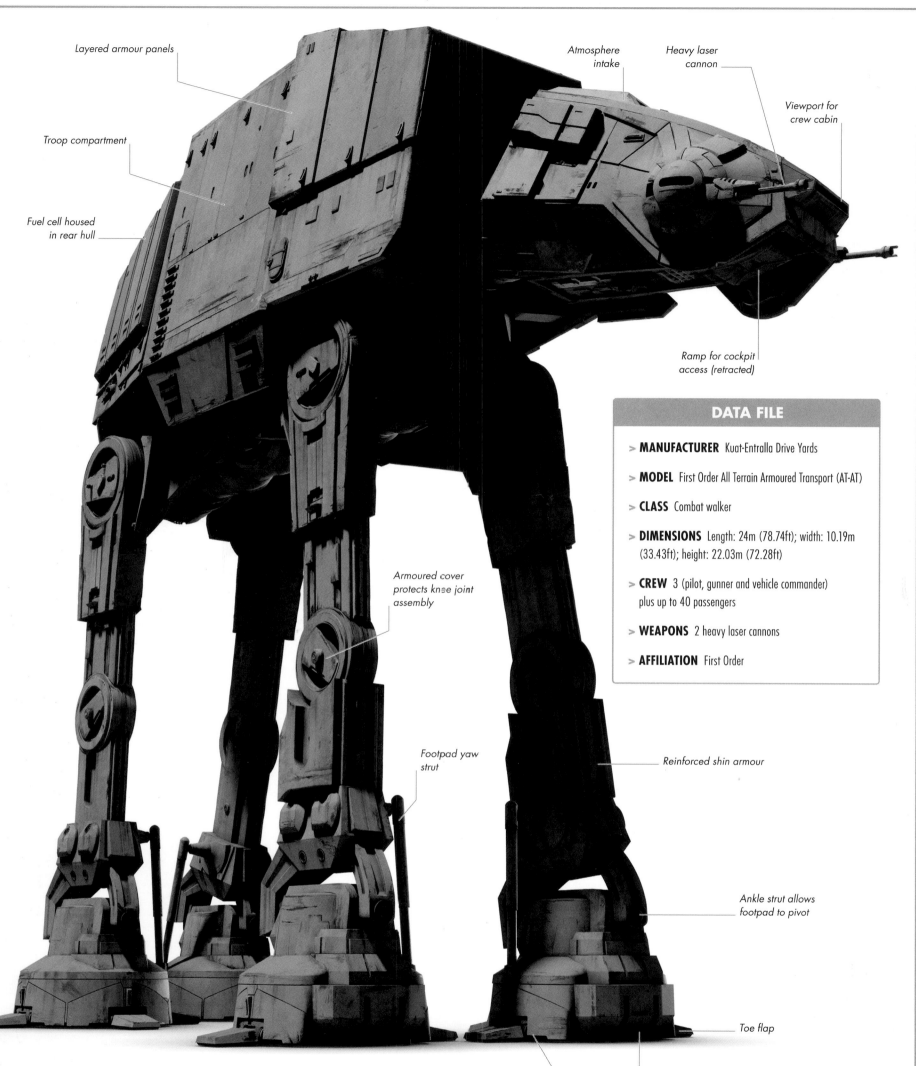

Layered armour panels

Troop compartment

Fuel cell housed
in rear hull

Atmosphere
intake

Heavy laser
cannon

Viewport for
crew cabin

Ramp for cockpit
access (retracted)

Armoured cover
protects knee joint
assembly

Footpad yaw
strut

Reinforced shin armour

Ankle strut allows
footpad to pivot

Toe flap

Terrain
sensors in
footpad

Reinforced
toe for smashing
aside obstacles

DATA FILE

> **MANUFACTURER** Kuat-Entralla Drive Yards

> **MODEL** First Order All Terrain Armoured Transport (AT-AT)

> **CLASS** Combat walker

> **DIMENSIONS** Length: 24m (78.74ft); width: 10.19m (33.43ft); height: 22.03m (72.28ft)

> **CREW** 3 (pilot, gunner and vehicle commander) plus up to 40 passengers

> **WEAPONS** 2 heavy laser cannons

> **AFFILIATION** First Order

AT-AT

The AT-AT was one of the most feared components of the Imperial Army, equally effective as a ground assault vehicle and a psychological weapon. The First Order has seen little need to change an effective formula, deploying AT-ATs according to longstanding Imperial procedure. Beneath its armoured skin, however, the latest incarnation of the AT-AT benefits from improved targeting sensors and speedier weapon recharge rates. Its toughened shell is different, too: lightweight materials are layered in a matrix that is stronger than Imperial-era armour, but no heavier.

RESISTANCE SHUTTLE

THE RESISTANCE RELIES on transports for any number of tasks, from ferrying equipment between bases to carrying command personnel to clandestine meetings with sympathetic New Republic bureaucrats. Formally known as U-55 loadlifters, these transports are unarmed, slow to manoeuvre and incapable of faster-than-light travel. Transport pilots know they are easy prey for any enemies, and rely on fighter escorts to travel the spacelanes in safety. The Resistance has larger transports, including a few ancient GR-75 cargo-haulers, but it has found U-55s simple to maintain and useful for a range of missions. These transports have served capably as mobile command centres, medical vessels and courier craft, with their versatility and stodgy reliability offsetting their lack of combat capabilities.

REPUTATION FOR RELIABILITY

The U-55 loadlifter is the latest model in a venerable line of transports – commonly used across the galaxy by everyone from planetary security forces to corporations and government ministries. U-55s are simple to operate and repair, and cadets learn to fly these reliable craft in military academies and the merchant marine. Their minimal defences are engineered for flight safety, offering protection against meteorite impacts, solar-flare radiation and other natural hazards.

Static discharge node

Atmosphere processing

Life-support ducting

Primary heat sink

Exhaust venting

Sublight ion engine

Sublight ion engine augmentation grill

Sublight ion engine thrust nozzle

Improvised shunt diverts ion flux

Power conduits for baffler

Backup emergency systems

Engineers nervously monitor baffler interface

Hastily installed flux tank forms part of "baffler" modification

BAFFLING THE ENEMY

The Resistance has hastily equipped many of its more vulnerable vessels – shuttles, transports, lifeboats and even escape pods – with jury-rigged baffler technology that makes them harder to detect. A young flight engineer, Rose Tico, created a prototype baffler to hide a Resistance bomber on a spy mission in the Atterra system, linking a droid brain with an assembly of engine baffles, shunts and fuel tanks. After Rose's creation successfully reduced the bomber's ion emissions and made its energy signature harder to detect, Vice Admiral Holdo ordered this "poor being's cloak" to be adopted throughout the fleet.

Repulsorlift medical stretcher

Hull reinforced against impacts and radiation

Artificial gravity generator

Passenger seating

Cova Nell, co-pilot

Flight deck

Forward viewports

Pamich Nerro Goode, pilot

Poe Dameron

Kaydel Connix

C-3PO

Starboard deflector shield generator

Large transparisteel cabin viewports

General Ematt

Fuel cells

Portside rear landing gear actuator

Reservoir locking valve for landing gear

Stabilisers for atmospheric flight

IMPROVISED ESCAPE

The old veterans among the Resistance's officers like to impress new recruits by telling harrowing tales of the Rebellion era: favourites include the Battle of Scarif, the evacuation of Hoth and the reinforcement of Thila. But the retreat to Crait strikes even these old hands as a desperate gamble. With the Resistance fleet low on fuel and unable to escape its First Order pursuers, Holdo flees for a forgotten bolthole established when the Rebel Alliance was still but a dream, ordering Resistance members to abandon their vulnerable capital ships aboard a flotilla of U-55 transports. The Resistance will need both bravery and luck to survive the day.

SKI SPEEDER

THE RESISTANCE HAS A TRACK RECORD of making ends meet with surplus New Republic warships, supplies obtained on the black market and carefully maintained equipment from the Rebellion era. But ingenuity gives way to desperation when a First Order strike force corners the Resistance on Crait. Frantic repairs to ancient, rickety ski speeders that predate the Alliance lead to the debut of Poe Dameron's "Reb" Squadron. The fragile-looking ski speeders were originally civilian sports repulsorcraft, up-armoured by long-gone rebel techs for use as patrol vehicles. These lightweight craft were never intended to take on anything bigger than the speeder bikes and ground vehicles favoured by smugglers and pirates – but they now stand as the Resistance's last line of defence.

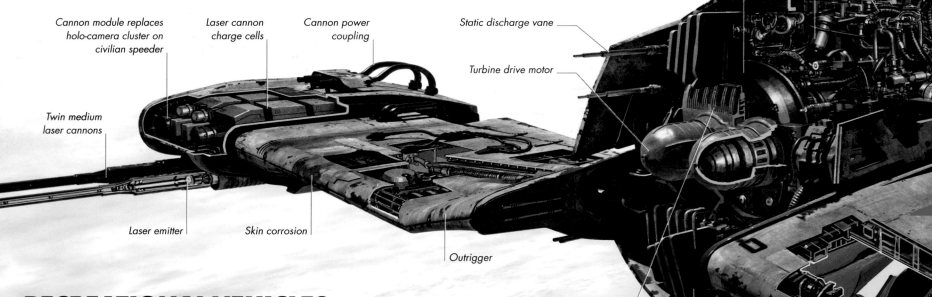

Insulated reactant fuel lines

Hybrid engine can also function in vacuum

Compressor

Fuel injector

Cannon module replaces holo-camera cluster on civilian speeder

Laser cannon charge cells

Cannon power coupling

Static discharge vane

Turbine drive motor

Twin medium laser cannons

Laser emitter

Skin corrosion

Outrigger

Turbine atmosphere intake

Heat exchanger grill

Terrain sensor

Halofoil shock absorber

RECREATIONAL VEHICLES

The early Empire witnessed a fad for asteroid slalom, a sport in which competitors sped along the surface of small asteroids, using them as springboards for high-speed turns and eye-catching stunts. The Verpine manufacturer Roche Machines produced the V-4 series of ski speeders, which boasted ventral mono-skis to keep the speeders anchored, and boom-mounted holo-cameras to record manoeuvres. Unfortunately, an undetected stone-mite infestation led to the devouring of several racers and their craft in the Orleon Belt Grand Slalom Finals – a tragedy watched live by a horrified galaxy. As bookings plummeted, Roche Machines cancelled production and sold off its inventory at slashed prices.

UNLIKELY BUYERS

With the asteroid slalom craze over, most of Roche Machines' ski speeders were scrapped. But a few found unlikely second lives thanks to tinkerers in asteroid settlements. Ski speeders were recast as exploration craft and transports, their outriggers adapted for mounting everything from scientific instruments to supply pods. Meanwhile, a rebel cell backed by Alderaanian credits adapted a number of ski speeders for use as patrol craft on Crait. The rebel techs attached laser cannons to the speeders' booms and added as much armour as the lightweight craft could accommodate.

CRIMSON CALLING CARD

Ski speeders were designed for use on asteroids, where there is enough gravity for repulsorlifts to engage, but not enough for true flight. They prove mildly terrifying to pilot in the heavier gravity of a planetary surface – the overcompensating repulsors threaten to launch the lightweight craft into the air with every bounce. The ventral mono-ski stabilises the speeder, ensuring its powerful engine supplies thrust and not lift, and cuts a groove in Crait's bright white layer of saline crust. Crimson crystalline dust gouged out by the mono-ski is caught by the engine blast, giving each speeder a defiantly gaudy red tail.

FAMILY RESEMBLANCE

Sizing up his first ski speeder, Poe Dameron complains that it's "a B-wing that can't fly". The squadron leader is closer to the truth than he knows: the ski speeder's cockpit pod, central engine and outrigger are mainstays of Verpine ship designs, which include the T-6 shuttle, the V-19 Torrent starfighter and the production model of the B-wing fighter. The B-wing line began with a prototype built by the Mon Calamari engineer Quarrie, who sought to improve on designs conceived by Verpine shipwrights.

Repulsor field thrust vector ring and rudder

Duraboard construction

Anti-turbulence cowling

Hastily repaired control cables

Wing fuel cells

Reactant mixer fuel lines

Auxiliary power generator

Cooling fan

Acceleration compensator

Cooling air passage

Cooling vents

Throttle lever

Halofoil mono-ski

Rhodocrosite dust

Targeting sensors

Steering column

Navigation computer

Navigation sensor spine

Ablative armour plating

Pilot controls

Kinetic shield projector

LAST STAND
Trapped on the barren salt flats of Crait and facing almost certain destruction, the surviving pilots of the Resistance charge their ski speeders straight at the First Order's invasion force.

SIZE COMPARISON

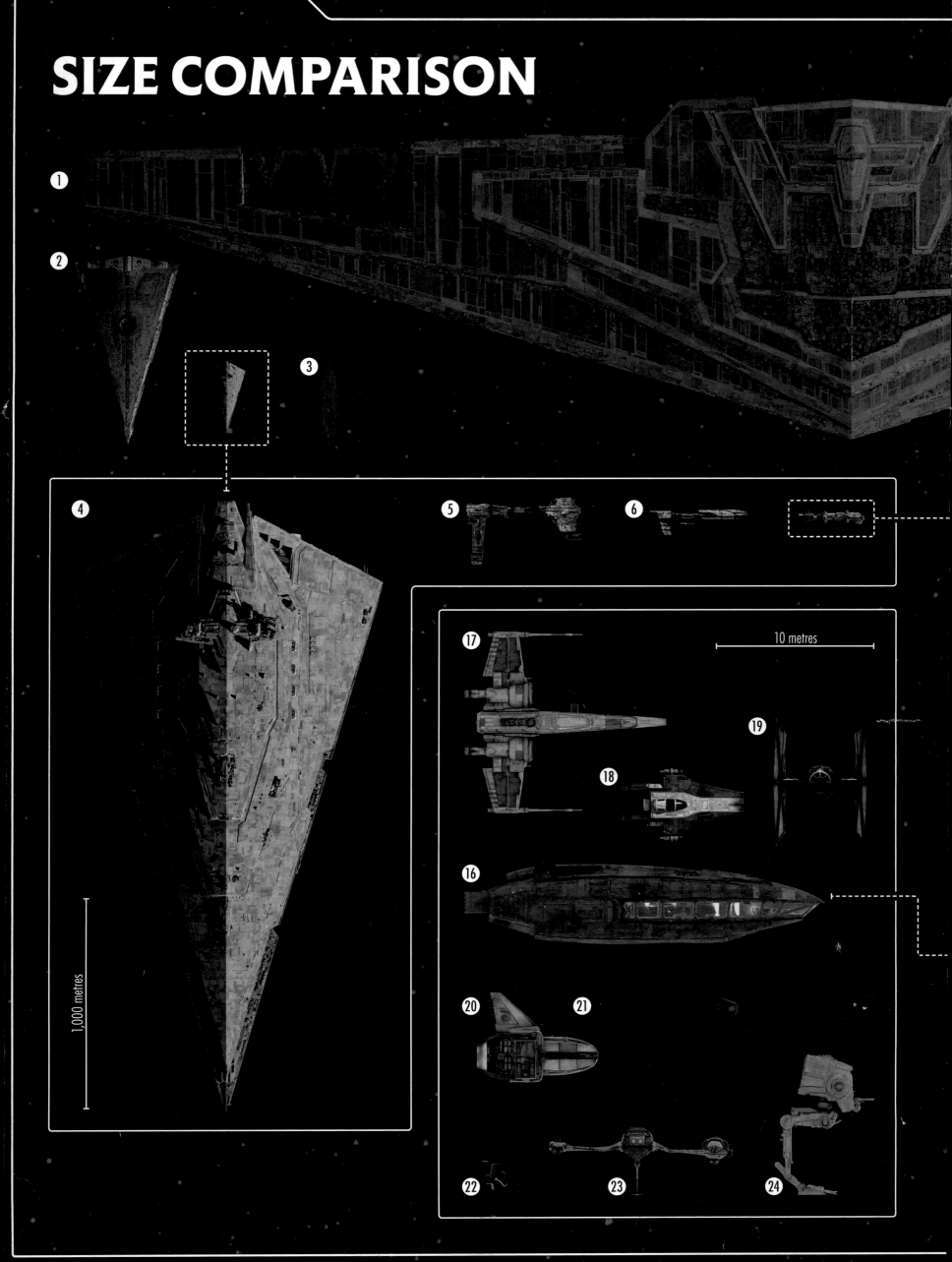

1

2

3

4

5

6

17

10 metres

19

18

16

20

21

22

23

24

1,000 metres

10,000 metres

1. *Supremacy* Width: 60,542.68m (198,630.84ft)
2. *Fulminatrix* Length: 7,669.71m (25,163.09ft)
3. *Raddus* Length: 3,438.37m (11,280.74ft)
4. *Finalizer* Length: 2,915.84m (9,566.4ft)
5. *Anodyne* Length: 549.17m (1801.74ft)
6. *Vigil* Length: 496.92m (1630.31ft)
7. *Ninka* Length 316.05m (1036.9ft)
8. *Millennium Falcon* Length: 34.52m (113.25ft)
9. *AT-M6* Height: 36.18m (118.7ft)
10. *Upsilon*-class shuttle Height: 37.2m (122.05ft)
11. *Libertine* Length: 52.92m (173.62ft)
12. MG-100 StarFortress Length: 29.67m (97.34ft)
13. First Order light shuttle Height: 18.31m (60.08ft)
14. First Order AT-AT Height: 22.03m (72.28ft)
15. AT-HH Height: 14.29m (46.88ft)
16. U-55 loadlifter Length 22.63m (74.24ft)
17. T-70 X-wing Length: 12.74m (41.8ft)
18. RZ-2 A-wing Length: 7.68m (25.2ft)
19. First Order TIE fighter Length: 6.69m (21.95ft)
20. Resistance transport pod Length: 7.73m (25.36ft)
21. TIE silencer Length: 17.43m (57.19ft)
22. Canto Bight police speeder Length: 2.98m (9.78ft)
23. Ski speeder Width: 11.5m (37.73ft)
24. First Order AT-ST Height: 8.89m (29.17ft)

100 metres

⑦

⑧ ⑨ ⑩ ⑪

⑫

⑭

⑮ ⑬

10 metres

ACKNOWLEDGEMENTS

Kemp Remillard: I'd like to thank Owen Bennett, David Fentiman, Simon Beecroft, Ron Stobbart, Sadie Smith, Tom Morse, Ruth Amos, Rachel Kempster Barry, Vince Venditti, Kristen Fisher, Julia O'Halloran and everyone at DK for making these books possible and having faith in me to continue illustrating the machines of *Star Wars*. Many thanks to Pablo Hidalgo, Phil Szostak, Brett Rector, Travis Murray, Sammy Holland, Newell Todd, Troy Alders, Leland Chee and everyone at Lucasfilm for their continued help and support in making these volumes. Special thanks to Cameron Beck and Chris Medley-Pole for the invaluable help with 3D assets. And of course, a giant thanks to Jason Fry for bringing these pictures to life with the written word. I'd also like to thank Kathleen Kennedy, Rian Johnson, George Lucas, Richard Chasemore and Hans Jenssen for making it all possible.

Lastly I'd like to thank my family in GA/NY, all of my good friends in San Francisco, Berlin, Seattle, Los Angeles, Athens GA and everywhere in between for all the support and encouragement. I couldn't have painted all of these tiny machine parts without you.

Jason Fry: Thanks to David Fentiman, Owen Bennett and Brett Rector for shepherding us; to Pablo Hidalgo, Phil Szostak and Leland Chee for helping fill in the blanks; and to Rian Johnson for giving us such a fun story to play with.

DK: We would like to thank Kemp Remillard and Jason Fry for their hard work in bringing these fantastic machines to life. Also thanks to Brett Rector, Michael Siglain and Sammy Holland for their invaluable assistance, and to Pablo Hidalgo, Phil Szostak, Leland Chee and everyone else at Lucasfilm who helped steer us in the right direction.

DK | Penguin Random House

Senior Editor David Fentiman
Senior Designer Owen Bennett
Creative Technical Support Tom Morse and Andrew Bishop
Pre-production Producer Marc Staples
Senior Producer Mary Slater
Managing Editor Sadie Smith
Managing Art Editor Vicky Short
Publisher Julie Ferris
Art Director Lisa Lanzarini
Publishing Director Simon Beecroft

For Lucasfilm
Senior Editor Brett Rector
Asset Management Steve Newman, Newell Todd, Gabrielle Levenson, Erik Sanchez, Bryce Pinkos and Travis Murray
Associate Technical Director Cameron Beck
Art Director Troy Alders
Story Group James Waugh, Pablo Hidalgo, Leland Chee and Matt Martin

First published in Great Britain in 2017 by
Dorling Kindersley Limited
80 Strand, London WC2R ORL
A Penguin Random House Company

10 9 8 7 6 5 4 3 2 1
001—298135—December/2017

Page design copyright © 2017 Dorling Kindersley Limited

A CIP catalogue record for this book is available from the British Library.

ISBN: 978-0-24128-107-9

Printed and bound in Slovakia

A WORLD OF IDEAS:
SEE ALL THERE IS TO KNOW

www.dk.com
www.starwars.com